D0573027

Feathers of Hope

Feathers

of

Hope

PETE DUBACHER,
THE BERKSHIRE BIRD PARADISE,
AND THE HUMAN CONNECTION WITH BIRDS

Barbara Chepaitis

excelsior editions

State University of New York Press
Albany, New York

Cover photo courtesy of Billy LeRoux.

Published by
State University of New York Press, Albany

© 2010 State University of New York

For information, contact State University of New York Press, Albany, NY
www.sunypress.edu

Production by Kelli LeRoux
Marketing by Fran Keneston

Library of Congress Cataloging in Publication Data
Chepaitis, Barbara.
 Feathers of hope : Pete Dubacher, the Berkshire Bird Paradise, and the
human connection with birds / Barbara Chepaitis.
     p. cm.
 Includes bibliographical references.
 ISBN 978-1-4384-3291-5 (hardcover : alk. paper) 1. Dubacher, Pete.
2. Berkshire Bird Paradise Sanctuary (Grafton, N.Y.) 3. Bird
refuges—New York (State)—Grafton (Town) 4. Bird watching—New York
(State)—Grafton (Town) 5. Human-animal relationships—New York
(State)—Grafton (Town) I. Title.
 QL676.56.N48C44 2010
 639.9'780974741—dc22

                                                              2009051685

10 9 8 7 6 5 4 3 2 1

To my husband, Steve Sawicki,
with gratitude for his flights of fancy and his safe landings.

CONTENTS

ILLLUSTRATIONS

Hope is the thing with feathers
That perches in the soul,
And sings the tune without the words,
And never stops at all,
And sweetest in the gale is heard;
And sore must be the storm
That could abash the little bird
That kept so many warm.
I've heard it in the chillest land,
And on the strangest sea;
Yet, never, in extremity,
It asked a crumb of me.

—*Emily Dickinson*

VICTORIA CROWN PIGEON,
PROUD AND VAIN

INTRODUCTION

Paradise Found

The Huma, also known as the "bird of paradise," is a Persian mythological bird, similar to the Egyptian Phoenix. It . . . is considered to be a compassionate bird and its touch is said to bring great fortune. . . . It avoids killing for food, rather preferring to feed on carrion. The Persians teach that great blessings come to that person on whom the Huma's shadow falls.

According to Sufi master Inayat Khan, "there is a belief that if the Huma bird sits for a moment on someone's head it is a sign that he will become king. Its true meaning is that when a person's thoughts evolve so that they break all limitation, he then becomes as a king. It is a limitation of language that it can only describe the Most High as something like a king."

—*www.newworldencyclopedia.org/entry/Phoenix_(mythology)*

Thou singest with so much gravity and ease;
And above human flight dost soar aloft
With plume so strong, so equal and so soft.
The Bird named from that Paradise, you sing
So never flags, but always keeps on Wing.
Where couldst thou words of such a compass find?
Whence furnish such a vast expence of mind?

—*Paradise Lost*, John Milton

I FOUND PARADISE in the mid-1990s by accident, not too far from Troy, New York.

I was at Grafton Lake with a friend I'll call Amanda, and we decided to explore a little further up the road, looking specifically for the Peace Pagoda, which she'd heard was a good place

1

to stop and have a picnic supper.

On the way we passed a sign that said "Berkshire Bird Paradise." I looked at Amanda and asked, "You up for Paradise?"

"Sure," she said. "Why not?"

We turned and drove down the road. It was, at first, a pleasantly winding country road, rolling past ranch houses from the 1950s, a few contemporary houses, a few doublewide trailers. Some had gardens with elaborate lawn ornaments in front. Some had rusted out cars. A mixed neighborhood. Then, another sign, hand-made, asked us to turn right down Red Pond Road. Here, the world kind of disappeared.

If the road to Hell is paved with good intentions, apparently the road to Paradise is not paved at all. It's dirt all the way, and bumpy and twisty, too. In summer, dust rises in your wake—I wouldn't want to try it in a heavy spring rain. With no further indication that we were headed the right way, we kept going on faith alone until, to our right, we saw a small herd of fallow deer peering at us from over a fence. Soon after that, we came to a driveway, and a weatherworn sign with an eagle on it. "Berkshire Bird Paradise," it said. This, we assumed, was it.

We parked and got out of the car. To our left, we heard what sounded like distant drumming. To our right, something clacked. In front of us, a gaggle of geese came storming down a walk, honking as they approached.

"This must be the place," Amanda said.

The geese faced us briefly, said something unmistakably scolding, and turned back where they came from. We saw a blue barn to our left, a blue house to our right, and gravel paths in front of us. We walked hesitantly down one of them, passing more than a dozen six-foot-tall wingless birds who flocked behind a fenced-in area to our left. I'd never seen birds quite like this before, with wispy, light-brown feathers and large, peering eyes. The drumming, I realized, was their sound, an almost purr that emanated from their long, curved throats. They trailed us as we walked, eyeing us closely, their expressions a mix of friendly curiosity and superciliousness: Hello there. Please do come right in, but mind you don't mess up the place. And did you bring anything to eat?

At first it seemed as if the birds were in charge. We saw no human creatures as we wandered down a path lined with enclosures that held startling cranes, brooding falcons, cooing pigeons, exotic ducks. We felt slightly illegal, trespassers on their territory. Then the enclosures opened up into a space between buildings, and we saw a woman with long auburn hair wheeling a baby stroller. In the trees behind her, a large crow cawed and flapped its wings. As she walked, it hopped and flew from branch to branch, following her. Finally, it soared out of the trees, and came to a gentle landing on her shoulder. She continued walking as it poked at her hair, until she disappeared from view behind the house.

Well then, I thought. This is indeed paradise, of a sort. Or a Disney movie. We kept walking, passing aviaries occupied by pheasants, more hawks, and owls. The area opened up and showed us woods, a pond, more trail.

Ahead of us was a fenced area, and behind the fence were the deer we'd seen from the road, as well as towering wooden structures like giant bird cages or tree houses on stilts. As we moved toward them, a rugged-looking dark-haired man in jeans and t-shirt came bustling toward us, offering a bright and slightly distracted smile.

"Hi," he said. "I was just checking the eagles. Come in, come in," he gestured to us, and we followed him into the fenced-in area. "I had to put this up so the deer don't wander. Get themselves shot around here, right? Hey—lemme show you the totem pole. I just finished it. For my daughter, right? Oh, I'm Pete," he added, as an afterthought.

We trotted after him, pretty certain he wasn't an axe murderer or anything. I don't remember if we asked him who he was in relation to this place. Maybe we assumed it was his place, or at least that he knew enough about it to show us around.

And, of course, we didn't have much time to think about it, because we were soon walking among the deer we'd seen from the road. They gazed at us with mild forebearance. One of the large birds joined us, close behind Pete, drumming softly. It poked gently at Pete's back. He ignored it and kept talking.

"Don't mind the emus," he said. "They won't bother you."

"Emus?"

"I have a bunch. Here's the totem pole," he said, pointing ahead. "I made it to remind my daughter to believe in her dreams. That she can do anything she puts her mind to."

We stopped and looked up. And up. The totem was an old telephone pole, intricately carved. There was a serious crescent moon at the base, topped by a powerfully rayed burnished sun, over which two carved bald eagles greeted each other lovingly.

ELIZABETH'S
TOTEM POLE

Brightly painted and intricate in detail, it was an impressive piece of art.

"Wow," I said. "You made this?"

"Yeah, I carved it. Pretty big job," he laughed. "I don't know if I would've done it if I knew what I was getting into. But you have to try these things, don't you?"

Though I didn't realize it at the time, that statement sums up Pete Dubacher's life philosophy. With that approach, you're almost bound to get yourself in a place where, for instance, you operate a bird sanctuary that permanently houses over a thousand birds, your life devoted to breeding and caring for birds who can't live in the wild.

For my part, I was enchanted, and I remain enchanted by both the human and nohuman inhabitants of the Berkshire Bird Paradise to this day. That's due, in part, to a long and complicated history I have with birds, but also due to the fact that it is enchanting to witness someone live a dream like Pete's, which earns no fame or glory in the current cultural model, but which is apparently completely in sync with his soul, his authentic nature. Pete dared to take the road that suited him best, and he's been successfully walking it for thirty-five years. How many people do that?

His efforts have earned him a national conservation award from the Daughters of the American Revolution, and letters of praise form President Clinton and George Pataki. Ward Stone, wildlife pathologist for NYS Department of Environmental Conservation says he's the Mother Teresa of the wild bird world. But most local people know him simply as The Bird Man.

Plenty has been written about movie stars and serial killers, powerful politicians, baseball players, and wealthy men. But we often ignore the importance of the work done by people like Pete Dubacher, people whose lives are useful, interesting, and sometimes a little strange. At one visit, I arrived at the bird sanctuary with group of college students to find Pete cheerfully unloading dead possums from the back of a truck, a recent contribution of roadkill from New York State Department of Environment Conservation (DEC). Enchanted as the place is, it exists very much in the real world, and Pete has to deal with problems of food and shelter for his family of humans and birds, just like everyone else. The Berkshire Bird Paradise reminds us that even though the most eccentric dreams can come true, they take an awful lot of waking work.

When I started writing this book, I hoped to find out why anyone would take on such an enormous task, and how they managed to keep it going. As I went along, more questions grew up around that, such as how and why does anyone develop a love of birds? In search of answers, I spent time following Pete around, and I spoke with many other people—birdwatchers, bird educators, wildlife aficionados, and ordinary people who had stories to tell about their own involvement with birds.

This book, then, explores the history and daily functioning of the Berkshire Bird Paradise and the man who created it, as well as the larger human connection to the things with feathers. By that, I mean both birds and the aspirations they often represent. I hope readers will feel the breath of wings at the back of their necks, inspiring them to their own flights of dreams and the insanity of true love.

Because, as Milton and Dante would confirm, love is ultimately what Paradise is all about. Even if it's all for the birds.

ONE

Hatchlings

A Bearer, Begetter speaks: "Why this pointless humming? Why should there merely be rustling beneath the trees and bushes?"

"Indeed- they had better have guardians," the other replied.

As soon as they thought it and said it, deer and birds came forth. And then they gave out homes to the deer and birds:

"You, precious birds: your nests, your houses in the trees, in the bushes. Multiply there, scatter there, in the branches or trees, or the branches of bushes."

—*Popul Vuh*

7 A.M., *Altamont, New York*

LIGHT STRUGGLES THROUGH a covering of clouds and makes its way into my room, my eyes. Time to get up. I have a morning class to teach, Public Speaking for college students, followed by meetings and errands, and then I'll head out to the Berkshire Bird Paradise, where I'll stay the weekend to trail after Pete Dubacher and witness his daily routine with the birds.

My own routine starts with getting myself out of bed—no easy task. I'm a night owl, and an early morning class is the scourge of my life. The only compensation is that I often get to see the sun rising at the edge of the Heldeberg escarpment, with the last stars still lingering where the indigo horizon begins to turn gold and pink. There's still plenty of pretty out here on the border of Albany and Schoharie counties.

7

I creep to the window, scrunch back the curtain to look out over the land.

There's no frost today, though it's been a chilly October so far. The open patch of grass that leads to the woods behind our land is still green, my nasturtiums aren't wilted yet, the pond my husband dug still has frogs. I hear the morning caw of the ravens that take their breakfast at our compost pile. One of them opens large wings to swoop away.

As I follow its flight, I see motion at the pond. It's from something that blends perfectly with the silver gray environment until it moves. Then it becomes something large and gray, something ancient and unlikely, a visitor from Jurassic Park.

"Steve," I say to my husband. "The heron's here."

He mumbles into his pillow and rolls over. He's not a morning person, either. I get dressed and go downstairs, sneaking out onto our deck where I can get a better look.

Great Blue Herons are fairly common in our country neighborhood. Most of the people who live here have ponds, and there's a good balance of open field and wooded land all around the scattered houses. We've often seen them flying overhead, but they only started visiting our land a month ago, after we filled in the pond. The first heron to stop by is forever joined in my mind with how I got to write this book, and why I'll be going to the Bird Paradise later today.

What happened was this: I was pulling out of my driveway one Saturday in August, on my way to the grocery store. As I looked down the sparsely traveled road—checking for wandering dogs and cats as much as cars—I saw what looked like a large bird standing on the grassy verge a few yards away. I stopped, peered, pulled my car back into the driveway and turned it off, then walked over to investigate.

Standing there, looking rather forlorn, was a Great Blue Heron, about three feet tall. A juvenile, I figured, since adults are about a foot taller, and have more marked plumage. When I approached, she ducked her head shyly and backed up, but didn't fly away. A neighbor's truck went by, and she still didn't take off. I went and got Steve.

"Huh," he said when he came back with me. "Look at that. Must be a fledgling."

"She's not flying," I said.

"How do you know it's a she?" he asked.

I shrugged. "I don't. But I know she's not flying, so something must be wrong."

He sensed my tendency to intervene. "Let it be," he advised. "It—okay, *she* knows what to do."

A little reluctantly, I went on my way to the store. When I returned, and the bird was still there, I approached her again. She didn't seem sick or wounded. Just very still. "Listen," I said. "If you need help, come to the yard, okay?"

I went back into the house, and within half an hour when I looked out the window, there she was, standing quietly in our strawberry bed.

"Look," I told Steve. "We have to do something."

"Call Pete," Steve suggested. "Get his advice."

Pete Dubacher was my go-to guy for all the frequent bird events I've had in the last fifteen years or so. Since my first trip to his sanctuary, I'd been back many times, sometimes bringing my college students to work, sometimes just for my own pleasure. I'd also done some radio interviews with Pete around my novel, *These Dreams*, which has as one of its settings a bird sanctuary loosely based on his.

When I got hold of him and told him about the heron, he said, "Oh, yeah. Juvenile herons. I had one of those recently. Tangled up in fishing line. Maybe this one got kicked out of the nest because something's wrong with it, or maybe it left too soon. Either way, it probably doesn't know how to feed itself. You'll have to get food into it quick or it'll starve. Might be too late already. But just get a blanket over it, then bring it in. Do you have any fish? Mush it up, and stuff some right down the throat. Don't just put it in the mouth. Get it in the throat. They swallow whole trout, y'know? Oh—wear safety goggles. If they're scared they go right for the eyes."

I reported that unreassuring advice to Steve, and we went outside to stare at the heron. She was pitiful, all hunched up, a lost little girl.

"We don't have to try," Steve said. "You know how you'll feel if it—she—dies."

I sat on my deck and thought about that. I did know how I'd

feel, because I'd felt that way every time I had a failed bird rescue, and in fact, all my bird rescues failed. Often I felt like a kind of Charon, my job only to ferry birds across the River Styx to the underworld. One after another, they hopped into my life, stayed briefly, and died. I'd never had the chance to witness that flight away which should be the culmination of a rescue effort. And every death felt worse than the one before, an accumulation of failures that weighed heavily on my heart.

I also felt that way every time I got a rejection on a book or story, in spite of all the ones that have gotten published. No failure was ever anything to me except personal and deeply felt. My emotional barometer recognizes no other setting for these things.

And lately I'd been thinking that maybe it was time to stop trying quite so hard, for birds and books, for many things. I was at a crossroads in my career. A teaching job I'd loved was closed down by administrative fiat, a series of books I'd been working on were proving difficult. I sought something new for my life.

And what, after all, was the point of beating myself up? All current wisdom says that you should follow your bliss, not your pain. That you'll know when something's right because it will come easily. Though I was raised Catholic and spoon-fed a philosophy of suffering for the greater good, lately I'd been trying hard to embrace a more New Age attitude of manifesting what you want in material reality, following points of least resistance rather than banging my head into walls.

I could make a good start by letting this bird go. The local coyotes would put an end to her story, and I wouldn't have to bear witness. Nature would do what it does, and I could get on with my day.

But staring at the young heron, her sadly hunched shoulders, her beak tucked to one side and her eyes half closed, I felt something important stirring within me. Some essential message about my own authentic nature.

This is a sad bird, and she needs comfort, regardless of your neuroses, the message said. And you are someone who tries. That's who you are. That's what you do. You might as well get on with it.

I sighed. Deeply. "I can't leave her," I said to Steve.

Steve sighed just as deeply. "Yeah," he said. "I know."

We got a blanket, and easily caught the bird, who made no struggle against us. We brought her inside and set up a place in the cellar where she could rest quietly, with a blanket under her, and surrounded by a large tomato cage partly covered with another blanket. I microwaved my best frozen flounder, and as Steve held the bird, I got a goodly amount down her throat.

We went down later in the night and repeated the proceedings, and once again before we went to sleep. By the second feeding, she seemed more interested, a little more perky in receiving her food. The thing with feathers, which Emily Dickinson calls Hope, took up a perch in our souls. We went to sleep feeling it stir.

And when we got up in the morning to check on our visitor, she was a huddle of feathers in a nest of cloth. She'd died in the night.

I felt all the old pain of failure, of frustration, of longing. My heart ached for what would not be. Steve, just as sad, patted my shoulder and tried to give comfort when he needed it just as much. She was a beautiful bird, and we both longed to see her grow up, spread those great wings and take to the sky. And I had no one to blame for how I felt except myself. I'd taken this on knowing the possible consequences, and here they were. Hope flitted off its perch and moved on.

I laid her body to rest with all due ceremony, grieved my grief, and thanked her for the visit, apologized for my failure. I told her I wished I could have done better by her.

I was shaken up by the incident, and that night I went to sleep saying small prayers to whatever angels watch over the spirits of birds, wishing her a good journey. I also said a few prayers for myself, to whatever gods look out for fools. Send me on the path that's right for me, I asked. Send me in the direction of what I truly love.

The next morning, I woke to a call from Pete Dubacher, who told me he'd just had a conversation with an editor. She was interested in a book about the Berkshire Bird Paradise.

"You know me," Pete said. "I can't sit still long enough to write a grocery list much less a book. But I told her I know someone who can write it. She wants you to call her." He gave me her name and phone number, and thus, this book project was born.

Later that day, for the first time, an adult heron soared to a majestic stop at our pond, and has been visiting regularly ever since.

Granted, I have a long history of strange interactions with wild birds aside from my failed rescues. There was an owl that led me home when I was writing a fantasy novel about a group of people being led by an owl. There was a flock of bluebirds that once followed me home from a neighbor's house, after I told them I wished they'd come to my yard and visit. And there's much more, too strange to be called coincidence. But this conjunction of events was a bit much even for me. Still, at least one of my prayers had been answered, because I do love birds, and was glad of the opportunity to explore that interest further. The Berkshire Bird Paradise, which I associate with even stranger synchronistic events, seemed the perfect place to start.

I had many questions about the connections between humans and birds in general. It's easy enough to say you love birds, but why? Because they sing? So do iPods. Because they're pretty? So are Ferraris. I wanted particulars. I also wanted to know more about why Pete chose his peculiar path, how he manages to sustain it both financially and emotionally, because if I'm born to try, Pete is born to try harder. Much harder, and seemingly with a great deal more faith than I have. Also with a great deal more success where birds are concerned. The thing with feathers seems to perch eternally in his soul.

I've been wondering why that's so for him. Upbringing? Genetics? Good nutrition? The stars? He says he has a special birthday, June 21st, the longest day of the year. When he tells me this, I laugh and say, "Certainly the longest for your mother," and he agrees.

He was the firstborn, and at the time his father was working out of Honolulu Airport, as a chef for United Airlines. The year was 1948, and Hawaii had not yet achieved statehood, nor was the area as built up as now. He lived with his mother and father on the Wilder Estate, where they rented what was called the servant's quarters. That, he says, was way out in the wilderness back then, with no neighbors except animals and birds. He was the only child for the first eight years of his life, and for entertainment, he went exploring.

The estate was filled with flowers, unusual birds, waterfalls—all the flora and fauna a curious young boy could want. He remembers being fascinated by a particular kind of lizard that would detach its tail when you grabbed it, a built-in escape hatch that continued to wiggle on the ground after the lizard fled. He'd go looking for them, not just to pull their tails but also to watch them lay their eggs, watch the eggs hatch, and watch the tiny lizards scuttle away.

On occasion the family would go to the beach and comb the shore for shells, for life of all kinds. "I think we all have that inherent desire to explore, whether you're walking a path in the woods or a city street or a beach," Pete says. It's an impulse that never left him.

When he was eight, his mother had another son, and less than a year after that his father was transferred to New Jersey. It was, Pete says, a difficult transition. New baby, new home, new school. After the balmy weather and wilderness of Hawaii, he was now acclimating to Jersey winters. Later, another brother and sister were born and the family moved to Long Island, but they also purchased a summer home in Grafton, New York, where there were horses and chickens and gardens and woods. Peter always preferred that kind of environment to the city, which had too much noise, too much jarring motion for his tastes.

His urge to explore continued, though, and he planned to go to Europe after high school to pursue the same career in cooking he'd seen his father practice all his life. But in 1967 the draft was in effect, and young men of draft age weren't allowed out of the country without a lot of fuss, so Pete decided to use the system rather than fight it. In November of that year, he joined the army.

"I just went down to the recruiter and said I want to join," he tells me. "I figured I might as well get it over with. The recruiter almost had a heart attack. In those days, most guys were trying like hell to avoid the draft."

He remembers his father telling him, "Don't be a dead hero." Realizing he might get himself killed, he decided the only thing to do was make the most of his experience, whatever it was. He did what he continues to do. He paid attention, studied his surroundings, and performed to the best of his ability. As a result, during his basic training an officer approached him and asked what his educational background was.

"Sir," he said, "I only have a high school diploma."

"Only?" the officer said. "Most guys here don't have that. You're a leader."

So he was sent to take courses in leadership. Similar to officer candidate school but for noncommissioned soldiers, he remembers it as hard work, with lots of spit and polish. He emerged from the program as a sergeant, in charge of a platoon of mostly black and many illiterate young men.

"It was quite an experience," Pete says. "Here I was, nineteen years old and telling these guys my own age what to do. And you had to be careful. Lots of these guys had short fuses."

Yes, I thought, and they had guns. Quite an experience for a recent high school graduate. He was apparently up to the task and was sent to cooking school as well, then ultimately assigned to a unit in Panama, at the headquarters for Southern Command. The base overlooked Panama City but was surrounded by open land and rainforest. Nearby was a tunnel into a mountain where radar equipment was kept and classified work went on.

There he spent some time cooking in a mess hall, until word got around that he was doing very well. Then a general interviewed him to work on his staff, and he ended up as a Specialist 5 in the signal corps, which handled communications.

"That's where they sent all the smart people," Pete says. "I remember one kid who came in with a 4.0 GPA out of college. He was a genius. They did all this crypto work. The stuff they kept quiet."

He says the position was kept quiet as well. He was almost like a civilian, which was good, but also an eerie feeling. People would ask him what he did, and he couldn't say. But Panama was a good place to get his exploration fix, both in the rainforest surrounding the base camp and in Panama City itself, where he had his first experiences with bird rescues. At the open-air markets, among the sold fruits and vegetables, he'd see cages of parrots, finches, and other birds he couldn't name, for sale at a quarter apiece. Since the average person there earned two dollars on a good day, this was a pretty substantial business.

Pete felt bad for the little creatures, trapped, caged and sold. But he also felt sorry for the people. He was in the midst of a level of poverty he'd never witnessed. He'd see children digging in garbage cans, looking for something to eat, people living without running water in shacks. Then he'd see beautiful birds dead in their cages, or looking like they wouldn't live much longer. It was difficult to know who to feel the most sorry for.

His solution was simple, and very in character. He'd make a deal with the sellers to buy a bunch of birds for a few dollars, then take them back to the rainforest areas behind camp and set them free. At his salary, redemption was a pricey hobby, and his officers told him he was out of his mind, but he couldn't stand by and do nothing. He kept buying the birds, and setting them free.

His sympathy extended to other creatures as well. One day he saw a beautiful ocelot in a bamboo cage, panting from stress and heat.

"It was hot as hell, and here's this poor ocelot, and they're such beautiful creatures, right?" he says. "So I asked the man, how much you want for that thing, and he tells me seventy dollars. I couldn't believe it. And I sure couldn't afford it."

Pete tried bargaining, but the man wouldn't budge. He didn't have anywhere near that much, so he went back to base and started asking the other men if he could borrow some money. "I told them it was a loan, and when they found out what I wanted it for everyone gave something. Then a bunch of them came with me and we bought the ocelot and set it free in back of the base. Everyone was really happy about it, you know? They all felt like they did something good. And nobody wanted their money back."

That incident taught him something that's followed him throughout his life: people, he learned, feel good when they do something good for another creature. And generosity breeds more generosity around you. He's operated on those principles ever since.

While in Panama, he also had time to explore the more remote areas of the region. He'd go exploring on the other side of the canal, near Rio Hato, with the San Blas Indians who lived there. They called him "Jungle Boy" and thought he was a little crazy, always going after butterflies and lizards, always wanting to know about the creatures who occupied this world he'd stumbled into.

"They're small people—under five feet, mostly, but they had a wealth of knowledge. I learned a lot from them," Pete says. "They kept me out of trouble, too. I would've killed myself on my own, probably."

On one occasion he was trailing an anteater, curious about an animal he'd never see elsewhere. It started up a tree, and Pete continued after it, grabbing it by the tail. It was so strong, it started dragging him up with it, and he was willing to go, but one of the Indians grabbed his arm, shouting, "Let him go! Let him go!"

Pete was pulled back and the Indian pointed to the anteater's heavily clawed feet. "He said if that anteater grabbed you with one, it was full of bacteria, stuff that'd kill you," Pete remembers. "The guy saved my life."

Pete's time in the army was filled with those kinds of events. He saw toucans standing at the tops of trees, and huge flocks of parrots whose tattering sound could be heard for miles as they approached. He saved table scraps to feed the marmosets that came to the back of the general's house after breakfast. Later, he'd see them for sale in the market at twenty dollars apiece. As a result his memories of military service were quite different from many other Vietnam veterans.

"You gotta ask yourself sometimes why it is that you managed to survive all the craziness of life," he says of that time. "I mean, so many good people die young, so am I just a no-good bastard that I made it through? Or is there something I'm supposed to do?"

At a time when so many men faced the horror of combat, Pete ended up rescuing birds and feeding marmosets. Of all the experiences he could have gotten from the army, he'd found, or been found by, the ones that would best prepare him for what he'd do when he got out. He has the wisdom to appreciate that, and he's the kind of person who wants to give back even more generously than he's received.

By the time he left Panama, he already belonged to the birds.

And for the time being, on this chilly October morning, so do I.

I'm hoping that what I learn about Pete's life will also inform my own. Maybe I'll finally figure out all those failed bird rescues, or even do better next time. Maybe I'll come to understand the strange interactions I've had with birds. Maybe I'll find other people who have had strange interactions of their own.

I toss my bags into the back seat of my car, and give another look toward the pond. The heron stretches its neck, takes long steps forward, spreads its impossible wings, and takes to the air. It seems a good omen for the day.

TWO

Flight

The world offers itself to your imagination,
Calls to you like the wild geese, harsh and exciting—
Over and over announcing your place
In the family of things.
—Mary Oliver, *Wild Geese*

THERE ARE ALMOST ten thousand different species of birds in the world, seven hundred in North America alone, though not all are native. The ubiquitous starling, for instance, was imported from Europe by an industrialist who thought it would be nice to have all the birds Shakespeare mentioned in his plays in Central Park. Approximately eighty were brought to the New World, and now there are 140 million. You've probably seen them gather by the hundreds in noisy congregatiosn in the trees, where they remind me of chattering teenagers in a high school cafeteria. Sometimes, also like teenagers, they suddenly rise from the branches en masse and take flight, moving in a shadowy cloud of sound to another tree, talking all the way.

I suppose their numbers can be seen as a tribute to the power of the written word. Or, to the power of ancient creatures willing to eat anything from insects and bread to McDonald's happy meals flung casually out of car windows.

When I was growing up in Hudson, New York, we had plenty of starlings in our neighborhood, along with sparrows, crows and robins, and every summer included at least one baby bird rescue. My sister and I would find their rejected nestlings in our yard, lying at the bottom of a tree, their mouths opening and closing in silent appeal for food. We'd get a shoebox and some old rags and we'd make a nest of sorts, settle in the featherless, flopping body. We'd feed it white bread soaked through medicine droppers, fascinated by its voracity. They were gruesome little things, with huge heads and closed eyelids, veins pulsing through transparent skin. Tiny monsters that would someday become birds.

Our parents would say we should leave them alone and let nature take its course, but we had no idea what that meant, exactly. Or maybe we just saw ourselves as part of the course nature took rather than something separate from it.

We'd watch over each tiny hatchling carefully, feed them enormously, and call our friends in for the funeral rites when they died. Of course they all died, usually within a day. Baby birds really don't like having Wonder bread soaked in milk force-fed to them through medicine droppers.

Our funeral rites were elaborate, and we'd call in whoever was available in the neighborhood to attend. We'd place the Recently Deceased in a shoebox decorated with crayon drawings, and we'd solemnly cover the body with violets and dandelions gathered from our yards before putting the top on it. Rosaries in hand, we'd process around the yard to a hole we'd dug, then stop to say some ritual words before laying it to rest. Afterward, one parent or another would provide a funeral feast of cookies and milk, or fluffernutter sandwiches, or fried zucchini flowers and ginger ale.

I remember feeling those deaths more as frustration than grief, but I think those childhood rituals were a kind of practice for the larger letting go that's required of humans throughout their lives. From it, we learned that even our best efforts might not be good enough to get the results we wanted.

What I wanted, more than anything, was to see a baby bird feather out and take flight. I imagined it as a moment of intense freedom, and victorious bliss. Partly it had to do with a yearning to complete the mission successfully. But at an even deeper level, there's something fundamentally stirring about seeing a bird in flight.

Birds fly. That's one of their dominant characteristics. Humans, sitting at the top of the food chain, took tens of thousands of years to figure out how to get off the ground, but birds sometimes take to the air days after their birth, and they don't need a ticket. Or luggage.

Humans have probably always wondered what it's like to defy the pull of this massive planet, which keeps us bound to daily matters of work and bills and all the necessities of earthly life. If you fly, do you leave those worries behind? Is it similar to being an angel, occupying air and land, the celestial and earthly places? Birds have mastered the trick of living in the grittiness of daily life as well as the airy realm of the spirit.

Once, as I was driving along a country road, I saw a hawk swoop down from a nearby tree, headed toward a ditch. The speed at which he plummeted made me certain he would crash, but he soared up from the ditch without pause, a snake clutched in one talon. He soared to a nearby tree and had his meal, not at all concerned when I pulled over nearby to watch.

It was a messy business, the ripping and shredding of flesh a stark contrast to that airy flight. When it was done, he took off from the tree and circled up, higher and higher, until he was no longer visible. Being human, it's impossible for me not to wonder what gods he spoke to, and what he had to say to them.

Creatures that take to the air have been around since the pterodactyl, but the first feathers didn't make their appearance until about 140 million years ago, during the late Jurassic period, with a creature called Archaeopteryx, who may or may not have actually flown. One theory holds that Archaeopteryx lived on the ground, and used its wings only to help capture its prey. Another says it used them as a gliding lizard or squirrel does, for short flights from tree to tree.

What is not in doubt is that Archaeopteryx had feathers, which may have evolved from scales, and which are made of keratin, the same stuff that makes our hair and fingernails, animal fur and hooves. Fur and scales are all fine, but feathers are the best construct for getting airborne, and the capacity for flight allowed birds to escape predators as well as colonize the entire world.

Humans can also fly now, but not as easily as birds, and not without making a craft to fly in. Most of those are clumsy, noisy machines, which, quite frankly, terrify me. Birds, on the other hand, just lift wings and go.

Well, maybe it isn't quite that simple. Take-off requires a lot of energy, and birds accomplish it in a variety of ways. Some climb up on a cliff or a tree, launching themselves from a high place. Others, like pigeons, jump up vertically then pump their wings hard as they lean forward. Still others, like gulls and herons, use a runway method, getting a running start before take off.

Once airborne, birds can either glide, like hawks, or row, like geese. It takes less energy to let the wind do the work, but in either case, their streamlined build is crucial for getting the job done. Some birds even seem to realize this, and work to maintain it. The osprey, for instance, when it grabs a fish from the water, adjusts its hold to maintain a streamlined profile as it brings the fish to land. It actually appears to be surfing on the fish as it brings dinner home.

Regardless, like an Olympic athlete, birds make it look easy, and that ease captures our imagination, as well as our sense of longing. To fly, to be free. Or, at least, to watch another creature you've helped do that.

I'm not the only person who has yearned for that. Another is one of my former students, a young woman named Georgi Raimer. She's twenty-two, has pink hair, and wears a lot of leather, but her only piercings are her ears. If you saw her, you'd think her an unlikely person for bird care, but she's had her share of experiences with it.

She recently found a baby blue jay, a little downy-feathered thing. He ate enormously, (crushed worms, not wonder bread) and she didn't know exactly how much to feed him, but he was always screaming, mouth open, quickly recognizing her as the food person. She had him for about a week, and he seemed to be doing well. Then, one day she went in to feed him and he was dead. It was, she said, horrible.

"I was so sad because I didn't expect it. I thought he was doing really good, and I didn't think he was gonna die at all," she told me.

She buried him in the yard, made him a stick-and-twine cross, and was more upset about it than she thought she'd be. "If he'd died the first day I wouldn't have been so surprised," she said. "But when something that you're nurturing dies it's different because it's not only about the death of the animal, it's about your own character failings. I'm thinking, I can't take care of a bird, how can I take care of anything? What about kids?"

Some time after that when she was heading across University at Albany campus for class, she saw a baby bird, in the middle of an open grassy area between parking and campus podium. Another student stood near it, staring. She bent down, saw the downy feathers, and knew she had to do something.

So she went to the campus center and begged a soup bowl from the cafeteria, lined it with napkins, and with this impromptu nest in hand, went back and got it.

The bird went with her to the rest of her classes that day. In her creative writing class, the students, well, flocked around her, excited about their visitor. "They were like, oh look, a bird! A bird! Like they haven't seen that before," Georgi said. "The professor came over and just said, 'Oh. You have a bird. Let's get back to class.'"

She made an attempt to hide the guest in her next class, Critical Literary Theory, where she felt a baby bird might not be so welcome. "Creative writing, it's okay to be weird," she said. "Critical theory, not so much."

If the professor noticed, he never mentioned. Not even when it chirped. Still, it made her nervous, thinking she'd get in trouble for bringing something wild into the academic realm. "You don't know with a bird if it's going to just suddenly fly away. Wild things—or nature—don't belong in the classroom at the college level," she said, "I don't know how I'd justify it. What do birds have to do with Antigone?"

As a teacher, I'm guessing I'd figure out a way—hubris, other Greek myths about human attempts at flight, and so on. In fact I think it's sad that we don't refer to the wild world more often in academia. But that may only explain why I don't have a tenure track position. Certainly I understood Georgi's trepidation.

After a day of stealth, she brought her little brown bird home, and took care of it exactly the same as the blue jay. As he grew, she'd bring him outside to let him hop around. He didn't seem to be making progress, but then, she said, "One day, he just flew."

It turned out he was a brown creeper, so he did what creepers do. He flew into a tree, and then crept up the side. "I sat there for an hour, not sure what to do. After a while, I told him, 'Okay, you flew up there, so I guess you know what you're doing.'"

For Georgi, the moment redeemed what had happened with the blue jay. "I really was sad about the blue jay," she said. "I cried more than I should have, and I kept thinking 'c'mon, give me another chance. I can do it.' I really needed to find this one, and see it fly. It made me feel like maybe I didn't do anything wrong before. It made me feel really good."

For Georgi, the helplessness of baby birds moves her. They can't fly, and are vulnerable to predators. I asked her if there was anything in her nature that made her more empathetic to their vulnerability, and she said she supposed there must be, since she's seen other people just walk by baby birds. She can't name what exactly it is in her that makes her stop, however. "Maybe it has to do with growing up in the country," she mused. "Or maybe, the birds choose you."

I'm willing to consider that possibility. I remember a baby bird that followed me down Central Avenue in Albany, hopping and cheeping, ignoring everyone else except me. I took it in, fed it, and let it hop around after me for almost a week before I had a similar experience to Georgi's with the blue jay. Just as I had no idea why it followed me, I also had no idea why one morning I found it had died in the night. And I was, also like Georgi, really sad.

But Georgi's story brings something else home to me. Being human, we have the capacity to imagine and then empathize with the plights of others, human and nonhuman. Georgi feels her own vulnerability in an often cold world, and extends her care to others who are vulnerable. In caring for a small wild thing, then, she's also caring for what's wild and true in herself. At least some of our sorrow when that fails must be a kind of grief for the wounds our own wild nature takes within the confines of civilization.

Maybe wildness itself is the most vulnerable thing of all in this human-made world. And maybe, because we are creatures of imagination, when we see a wild bird take flight, a part of us experiences all that is wild and free about flight, along with all that is wild and free and true about ourselves.

Pete's relationship with birds must be slightly different, then, because most of his birds can't fly away. They are, like us, earthbound, and so even more vulnerable, lacking their primary evolutionary skill. In that sense, his life is a statement for the care of wildness at its most vulnerable. Maybe one of the enchantments of the Berkshire Bird Paradise is seeing a man who affirms the value of what's wild in this way, taking in these wounded souls, and saying, "This is valuable and worth protecting. I'll see that it has a home, no matter what."

In doing so, he is himself bound to their daily care. He can't remember the last time he had a vacation, and getting out to dinner is a struggle. But even though neither they nor he can fly away, they all seem more free than many people I've ever known.

 THREE

Landing

> Be like I, hold your head up high,
> Till you find a bluebird of happiness.
> You will find greater peace of mind .
> Knowing there's a bluebird of happiness.
> —*Bluebird of Happiness*, words by
> Edward Heyman and Harry Parr Davies,
> music by Sandor Harmati

Noon, Berkshire Bird Paradise

THE RIDE OUT TO the Berkshire Bird Paradise is pretty on an autumn day, when the world is golden and sunlit. The city of Troy drops away behind you and suddenly you're surrounded by fields where a few deer graze, hawks circling high above. The dirt road that leads to the sanctuary is dry and dusty today, and I'm glad for that. It can be, um, challenging when the weather is very wet. I asked Pete once if he ever tried to get the county to pave it, and he said no, he preferred it this way because it slows people down.

I pull into the parking area, lug my bag out of the car and stand looking around. I see no sign of Pete, and I know he won't be easy to find. He's built too ruggedly to say he flits, but he goes about his business at a pretty rapid rate, and he could be anywhere right now—tending a sick bird, stoking one of the woodstoves that heats the tropical bird aviaries, flinging bird seed around for pigeons.

I decide to take my bags into the house, called the Big House, where Pete's mother and father live, and where his daughter has a room upstairs. Pete and Betty Ann live "in the barn," Pete tells me. "That's what we call it." Their residence is attached to the barn, a smallish ranch/trailer. Nothing fancy. There is nothing fancy here at all, in human terms. The birds have cornered the fancy market.

Even the Big House is just a farmhouse, more than a hundred years old, ramshackle in layout, and with the feel of well-loved old about it. I knock on the door. Nobody answers. I knock again, then open it, entering an enclosed porch, where big boxes of old produce sit on a table, near wicker furniture and pots of flowers. I move to the interior door and knock on that, but still no answer, so I do what you do in the country. I open the door, stick my head in, and call out, "Hello?"

The kitchen is dimly lit, cluttered and homey. I hear a bird squawking, a television going, and sounds of motion. Then, a woman appears, walking slowly. She's tallish and thin, with soft white hair. She spots me and gives a radiant smile. A spare eld-

THE DUBACHER FAMILY ASSEMBLES, WITH CHIHUAHA.
LEFT TO RIGHT: BETTYANN, WILLIAM, CHRISTINE AND PETE.

erly gentleman appears behind her. This is Christine and William Dubacher, Pete's parents.

"She's here," Christine says to her husband. Then, to me, "Oh—come in. Yes, come in."

"I'm Barbara," I tell her, and she seems to expect me. I've never met Pete's family before and, given how he's turned out, I'm wondering what to expect. We all stand smiling at each other for a moment, and then Christine goes into motion, herding me into another room as her husband trails behind us.

We enter the living room, which has their bed in the middle of it, and she gestures at it impatiently. "I always have everything *just* so," she tells me. "I always make things pretty around, yes? But we have to sleep here since I've been sick, and I cannot *keep* it just so. I do not have the energy. I try to do things, and I have to *sit down*," she continues, clearly appalled with the notion. "It is how you might say, upsetting."

All of this said with the most vehement surprise and resentment. I recognize it. She's only a little older than my mother, nearing 90, and impatient with a body that no longer lets her to do what she's been doing her whole life. Ill health has kept her down this year. Heart trouble, surgery, teeth trouble. It's annoying as hell to her, and she sees no reason why it should be that way.

Still, she is as pretty as I hope to be at 87, with silky white hair up in a small bun at the top of her head, startling and vivid blue eyes, and a face that lights up expressively when she likes something and scowls just as expressively when she does not. She is a definite person. She continues telling me her health history, and it's clear that to her, these are problems that she should be able to solve. Problems are there to be solved, is the general attitude I glean. She's not complaining, really. Merely seeking solutions.

She gestures to an upholstered chair and I take it, thinking I might as well get some information from them before I go outside. Before I can say anything, there's a sharply piercing cry and I jump. In the doorway, William chuckles. "That's Scarlet," he says, and indicates a big white birdcage near the window. Inside is a medium-sized bright red bird.

"Is that yours?" I ask him.

"Oh, yes," he says, and takes her from the cage, holding her. I muse about people who resemble their pets. I'll come to find that William and his bird are both quiet, with occasional surprises. He lets me get a picture of the two of them, then puts the bird back in the cage and excuses himself, leaving me alone with Christine. "Now," she says. "This is good. Now we talk."

I'm ready with a question about Pete's childhood, but she starts first, and continues telling me her medical history, meticulously recounting a recent surgery.

I'm a little bewildered by her litany, not sure why she's telling me all this. Later, I'll find out that she had an appointment with a visiting nurse that day, and she thought that's who I was. Reasonably enough, she was telling me what she thought I was there to find out. Reasonably enough, I thought I was there to find out about Pete. That just shows you how far reason will get you.

Not realizing any of that at the time, I try to shift the conversation to my turf. "How long have you lived here?" I ask.

"We bought this place many years ago," she says. "We kept our horses here, and came in the summer with the children. But now, you see, I cannot go out and sweep the leaves. I want to know when I can get my teeth fixed."

I murmur sympathy, and ask if she liked birds as much as Pete does. Did he learn that from her?

Now she looks perplexed. She makes a sweeping gesture with her hand. "We always have love for all God's creatures. They should be loved, yes?"

Then she tells me more about her heart. We're both confused now, and both too courteous to ask the other what the hell is going on, so the study in communication failure continues unabated. After a while, a teenage girl comes tumbling into the room, ear firmly glued to a cell phone. She takes a look at the *mise en scene*, and retreats, but a chipmunk-size animal springs into the room in her wake, then ducks under the bed.

"Um, what was that?" I ask. I didn't think Pete rehabbed chipmunks.

"It is her puppy," Christine says and sniffs lightly. I sense disapproval, but I'm not sure if it's for me or the puppy.

"Puppy?"

"A chihuahua," she pronounces carefully. "Very shy. Now, I am hoping to have an appointment with the dentist next week, so my teeth will be fixed for Thanksgiving . . ."

As this continues, I begin thinking wistfully about how much easier it is to write fiction. My relationship with reality is vexed at the best of times, and I'm slightly panicked about my own capacity to do this job, or even get out of the room. Christine begins to look frustrated, and I decide it's time go find Pete. I excuse myself, tell her I'll see her later, and make my way back outside. When I leave, she looks as baffled as I feel.

Once I'm back outside, I take a moment to regain my equilibrium and give myself a pep talk. Just because you can't save a bird doesn't mean you can't write a book, I tell myself. Good Lord, you've had seven published. This is all easy. Piece of cake.

Back on track, I go in search of Pete, wandering the mazelike paths between the open bird houses and the duck pond, ducking under the arbor where Pete hangs plants of all kinds. The paths are lined with large clay pots that hold pretty little mosses, with little statues on top, or vining plants or orchids. I peek into one of the closed aviaries and see a table with rows of tiny orchids on it. Pete is also interested in plant life, and every year he adds something new to the place for flora as well as fauna.

That adds up to thirty-five years of developing the place, since he came back here about a year after he left the army in 1970.

First he went to Switzerland, where worked as a volunteer in a hotel at Interlaken and got experience in European cooking, as he'd planned to do after graduation. Once he was back in the states he decided to stay at the summer home in Grafton rather than going back to Long Island, where the rest of his family still lived. He got a job as a chef at The Jamaican in Latham, one of the ritziest restaurants in the area at the time, and he fully expected to work as a chef for the rest of his life.

But he was still interested in birds, and he kept chickens on the old farm. His interest in exotic birds and local wild birds continued, and he started to educate himself about them by reading everything he could about them, talking to people who knew about birds, and observing their behavior. He wanted to keep ducks and pheasants as well, and for that he needed a license. He applied and got one, and word got around that he was "good with birds."

As a result, he started getting calls from people who had injured owls and other birds of prey, but housing them required a different kind of permit, called a scientific lecters license. In order to get that, he had to have a game plan. A mission statement. A coherent idea of what he was doing, and why he was doing it.

He went to the Department of Environmental Conservation, and with the help of people like Ward Stone and Peter Nye, he developed a plan to start a bird sanctuary, for injured and disabled birds. It would be an educational facility as well, where school kids could come to learn about the birds.

"They thought it sounded like a good idea," Pete says. "So we got started. By 1983, we were really off and running."

And he's off and running still. As I walk the maze-like paths between aviaries, I notice a whole new home for crows and ravens, and two African cranes I hadn't seen before. They spot me and do their display dance, fanning their wings, bobbing their golden crests up and down, and giving an unearthly call. I also see a cage full of hawks I hadn't seen before, and I'm admiring them when rounds the corner, pushing a wheelbarrow full of wood.

"Oh, hi," he says. "You made it."

"I went inside first," I tell him. "I met your parents."

"Yeah. They're having a rough year," he notes, shaking his head. "Dad was diagnosed with lung cancer, and Mom had some heart problems. But they're holding their own right now. We moved them downstairs. Mom's not too thrilled about that, but we don't want her to hurt herself going up and down stairs." His face looks worried, and a little sad, not something you often see in him.

I'm struck once again by his inherent kindness. It can't be easy to care for aging parents along with more than a thousand birds and a teenage daughter, but he's not offering any complaints. Just concern. I feel a little guilty at not listening more to his mother.

"Did you see Elizabeth?" he asks. "She knows which room to put you in."

"She was on the phone," I tell him.

"Usually is," he frowns a little. Then, more concern. "Is that—uh—normal?"

"How old is she?" I ask.

"Fifteen."

"Very normal," I assure him. The frown goes away, and he offers a chagrined smile. He is father to a teenage girl, the strangest bird he'll ever fledge.

We move down the path, and I scoot ahead of Pete, holding open a battered door to one of the structures that house the "indoor" birds. The door looks recycled, and the entire structure is a baffling conglomerate of connected buildings that look like a cross between greenhouses and Quonset huts, made of wire and wood and covered in green canvas. Pete designed and built every one of them, with the help of a constantly shifting cadre of volunteers who come here from Cobleskill College or Massachusetts College of Liberal Arts (MCLA), or on their own. The materials are frequently recycled, sometimes gifts, sometimes purchased. Nothing here is wasted, and everything has the look of homemade ingenuity, a response to the necessities of both limited economy and bird needs.

"You built all this?" I ask as we enter.

"Yeah. An operation like this, you have to be an engineer, and a construction worker, and so on. You have to think of everything."

We wend our way down a narrow aisle between rows of chicken wire that house many different kinds of birds. Demure finches, a razor-billed curassow, a crested guan, and some exotic pigeons from New Guinea and Australia eye us briefly, then get on with their bird lives. Pete has been making it a point to bring in birds from further afield, especially if their habitat is threatened. From his Panama days he remembers seeing the start of slash and burn in the rainforest, and he knows it's gotten much worse since then. He hopes to be able to breed these birds, as well.

As we trundle on, Pete stops occasionally to look in on a bird.

"Look at that," he says, pointing to a bird with iridescent black, green, and blue feathers. It pecks around on its wood chip flooring, under the leafy plants and rugged tree branches that create its habitat. "You wouldn't think that's a pigeon, right? It is. Nikobar pigeon, from the Nicobar Islands. Their habitat is threatened so they're losing ground in the wild. I'm hoping they'll breed here. And there—that's a pigeon, too."

He points to chicken-sized bird feathered in elegantly under-stated gray, with a ruff of burnished brown and a crest of flowery blue feathers with white tips. Its eyes are bright red, and masked in black. This is a bird that knows how to look good.

"Victoria crown pigeon," Pete says. "Pretty neat, right?"

It is all that. It regards me for a moment, decides it prefers to chew wood chips, and moves away. Pete pushes the wheelbarrow through the whistles, coos, and clicks. On our left is an area with maybe a dozen birds that anyone would recognize as pigeons, these kept separate from the larger pigeon house for a variety of reasons.

"Some are injured, and recovering. Some really need a little less stress, less competition," Pete says. "They all have their own needs, just like humans. You just have to pay attention and you figure out what they are."

As we walk on, I'm willing to admit that I'm lost, or at least I lack any sense of where we are in relation to what I'd seen from the outside. This particular housing spans a quarter mile, Pete tells me, and it includes an Escher-like twisting of pipes on the ceiling that connect to a system of wood stoves. This is a rela-tively new project, again designed by Pete, to relieve the spiral-ing burden of fuel costs and provide maximum efficiency in delivering warmth to the tropical birds.

"You gotta remember, when the oil man delivers here, it's a ten thousand dollar bill," he tells me. "At least, it was last year. This year, it could be a lot more—gas is what, four dollars a gallon right now? But I'm waiting. I have a feeling that bubble'll burst, and I'm not buying until I absolutely have to."

This may be an enchanted place, but it's still in the world, and Pete has to cope with all the problems anyone else does in the northeast. Also, all the typical problems of a not-for-profit. He's understaffed, always has new clients coming in, and must rely on the kindness of others to gather in the $90,000 a year it takes to run the place. Ninety-nine percent of his income is from donations, mostly from people who have placed birds here. He has a website, but does no official fundraising, has no gala or PR program. Most people find out about him from other people, and somehow that all keeps working.

We enter the area where two of the woodstoves sit, waiting to be fed. Pete starts pushing wood into them. "I have to make sure they stay filled. So I go to sleep at eight, and if it's really cold out, I'm up at midnight getting more wood in. It's really important for these birds to stay warm."

I think of the Benedictine monks of the middle ages, who rose at midnight for Matins service, and again at dawn for Prime. "You're like a monk," I say to Pete. He laughs.

"I guess. It's all twenty-four seven, for sure. Right now, we're getting ready for winter, putting away all the stuff that can't be out in the cold, getting loads of wood in."

October is a transitional time. Every fragile thing, bird and plant, must go under cover, be kept warm. Even the clay pots have to be protected from the winter here. It's not only a lot of work, it requires a great deal of knowledge. Pete's formal education stopped at high school, so I ask where he picked up the know-how.

He shrugs. "I read. A lot. I got all kinds of books and just read them. Birdman of Alcatraz—that's been real helpful. And I talk to people, learn what I can from whoever I can. Then I spend time just watching. The birds teach you what they need, really, so a lot of it is just paying attention."

"Did you ever have a moment when you wanted to just . . . chuck it?"

At first, he looks like he doesn't quite understand the question. Then he shakes his head. "You see that they need you. You're aware that they'll die without you, and you can't just walk away from that. So you do what you have to."

I've asked him before why he does this, and he's said he loves being with the birds, or they need him, or it's better than a nine-to-five job. I consider briefly asking him again, just to see what he says this time, but it occurs to me that he'll give me the same look I give people when they ask me why I became a writer. That kind of choice isn't easy to articulate, because it's so deeply embedded in the spirit, in who you are. Writing is what I do. It's who I am. Pete cares for birds. It's what he does, who he is. Any other motivation must be parsed out by those who witness it from the outside.

But we are all connected to birds, whether we feel that or not. I look at their feathers and my own fingernails and know we're made of the same stuff. We're kin, sharing a planet. I wonder at their flight and return. I worry about the chickadees and nuthatches that huddle in my tree during snowstorms. How can they stand the cold? How many of them will starve or freeze? And because I feel that way, I'm more connected to the planet I share with them, more concerned to share it responsibly and well.

Environmental responsibility starts with love, I think. Feeling connected emotionally and imaginatively to the natural world is what inspires the energy to protect a place or a species. It's all about the love, really. At least, it is for me, and I know it is for Pete.

But what creates that connection, with wonder, mild interest, amusement, or with love, is multifaceted. For humans and birds, it's sometimes expressed as a spiritual bond, portraying birds as both the representatives and the teachers of our souls.

FOUR

Spirit Friends

And Elohim said, "Let the waters bring forth swarms of living creatures, and let birds fly above the earth across the firmament of the heavens. So Elohim created the great sea monsters and every living creature that moves, with which the waters swarm, according to their kinds, and every winged bird according to its kind. And Elohim saw that it was good. And Elohim blessed them, saying, "Be fruitful and multiply and fill the waters in the seas, and let birds multiply on the earth."

—*Genesis* 1:20

Truly in the east
The white bean
And the great corn plant
Are tied with the white lightning.
Listen! rain approaches!
The voice of the bluebird is heard.
—*Song in the Garden of the*
House of God (from the Navajo
corn-planting ritual)

Shia Muslims tell a story of the much-revered Imam Ali, from the day he was murdered. On that morning, as he left for the Mosque for morning prayers, his daughter Umm a Kulthum walked with him across the courtyard to see him off when a strange thing happened. Ali's pet geese flocked around him, quacking loudly. They tried to push him away from the door, grabbing at his clothes

37

with their beaks and pulling him back. The quiet, gentle geese had never acted in such an agitated manner. At this unusual behavior, Ali turned to Umm a Kulthum and said, "If something happens to me and you cannot care for them, make sure that they are released in the kind of wilderness where it is safe for them."

—*Oral Tradition, told by Anjum Jafri*

WHEN JESUS KNELT in front of John the Baptist for baptism, the gospels report that the Holy Spirit, in the form of a dove, hovered over him. And when Jesus left the apostles at His ascension into heaven, He sent the Paraclete for their continuing help. Many first graders have made the mistake of renaming this emissary of God the Holy Parakeet, a natural error, since it's often represented in art as a white bird.

Later Christian mythology uses a pelican as the symbol of the Eucharist, because it was believed that the female would pierce her own flesh to feed her blood to her young if no other food was available. The legend apparently grew from observing pelicans press their bills into their chest, in order to fully empty their pouch for their nestlings. The pelican is still the emblem of Corpus Christi College in Cambridge and Oxford.

This ancient use of birds as representative of exalted spirituality goes further back than Christianity, and crosses many cultures. In Hebrew scripture, a Raven brought bread to Elijah. In Aztec mythology, the great deity Quetzlcoatl is a feathered serpent, harking back to the earliest evolution of bird from reptile. Ancient Sumerian pictographs show bird-headed gods with wings.

Because birds occupy air, land, and water, they are easily seen as mediators between celestial and worldly realms, creatures that literally connect earth to sky. Accordingly, they've been viewed by many cultures as messengers of the gods, spirit guides and teachers for us poor earth-bound creatures.

My brother Peter, a Franciscan friar, would agree. He recently told me a story about attending at the deathbed of an old friend. When he left her, the doctor said she'd live for a few more days, but on the way home, Peter saw an eagle for the first time near his home in Middleburgh, New York. He immediately associated that sighting with the passage of his friend's soul, so he wasn't surprised when he got home to find a message waiting for him that his friend had died shortly after he left.

"Couldn't it be just coincidence?" I asked him. "Or just us humans creating meanings that suit us?"

"I suppose," he mused. "And really, I'll never know for sure. The truth isn't accessible to science right now. Some day there may be some kind of energy research to prove or disprove it, but does it matter? That kind of event, with the eagle, helps my heart and my spirit, and that's what's important."

My sister, Norma, agrees. Recently her friend Marie died, and after the funeral she went for a long walk near the Hudson River. "I said a little prayer for Marie," she told me, "and I just wished for some kind of sign that she was okay now. She had a hard life, and I hoped she found something better. And just as I said it, I saw this great big eagle perched in a tree. I never saw one before, and I walk there all the time. It made me feel better."

Maybe that kind of thing runs in the family. Or maybe we have enough old world peasant/pagan in us from our Italian and Lithuanian ancestors to notice it more than others. Certainly I've had too many strange bird events of my own to doubt that they offer us lessons of the spirit, no matter how you contextualize it.

For instance, quite a few years ago I was trying to figure out a relationship that was not going well. I was working hard to make it keep working, while he was doing pretty much what he wanted. Other women will know what I mean. During that time, I went to a garden nursery to get some flowers for my garden. As I was wandering through a greenhouse that seemed to explode with fuschias, I noticed a hummingbird flitting about, feeding at the flowers. I watched for a while, entranced as I always am by their improbable flight patterns, the improbability of their existence.

Suddenly, the hummingbird darted up toward the plastic ceiling, slamming into it. I was shocked, and then shocked once more as she did it again. And again. I kept watching, and she kept doing the same thing; flying up to the plastic, hitting it, twittering at it angrily, then aiming herself at it again.

Frightened for her, I got one of the staff and showed her what was happening. "You have to help her," I said, a little desperately. "Look what she's doing."

"Huh," the woman said laconically. "Yeah. Look at that."

"But—but shouldn't you get a net or something? Stop her? She'll kill herself," I sputtered.

"No. I don't think so."

"You don't?"

"No. We see them doing that sometimes. If you try and catch 'em, you end up hurting them. But see, after a while she'll get tired. When she gets tired, she'll drop down. When she drops down, she'll see the door and fly out."

"Oh," I said, unconvinced. "Oh. Sure."

But as we watched, she did just that. The woman was gracious enough not to say I told you so.

On the way home, I thought of the relationship I was ramming my head into. That day, I decided I was tired. Soon after, I dropped down and found the door.

Now, I'm sure there were many other signals in my life telling me that the right thing to do was end that relationship. I'm sure I had friends who said as much, in plain words. But watching the hummingbird's twittering frustration as she made her repeated attempts to escape through a closed ceiling while I was, all the time, aware that the exit was right there—right *there*—was an immediate and visceral lesson. People offered advice. The hummingbird showed me who I was at that time.

Of course, if that had happened at a different time, it wouldn't have had the same resonance, but it happened when I needed to see it most. And I did the work of paying attention, but the hummingbird gave me something to pay attention to.

You can chalk it all up to my novelist's talent for recognizing a good metaphor when I see one. You could say it's just coincidence. Or you could say it's synchronicity, as defined by psychologist Carl Jung. Note well, however, that he developed this concept after a strange incident with a bird. A dead bird.

What happened was this: In the fall of 1913, Jung was going though a very difficult period in his life. Having broken off professionally with Freud, he felt uncertain about the theoretical premises of psychology he'd been working with. He fell into a depression that was marked by unusually vivid dreams. One dream was of an old man with the wings of a kingfisher who was soaring across the sky.

Jung decided to paint this image, hoping this would help him understand its import. One day, while he was working on the painting, he went for a walk in his garden, and there he found a dead kingfisher. The discovery astounded him. Kingfishers weren't usually seen in Zurich, yet here was his dream, come to life—or death—at his feet. He realized that he'd been ignoring the important aspects of life that take place beyond rational dimensions of reality.

From this, he defined synchronicity as a meaningful coincidence in time of two or more causally unrelated events. Synchronicity is thinking about something, and then having that something show up. You're wondering how a friend is doing, and they call. It can also be a dream or vision that is reflected in an event that occurs at about the same time. It confirms a connection between our psyches and physical reality.

For Jung, this was not magic. It's simply what happens when an archetype—a form or pattern of a timeless object or image—emerges into consciousness, releasing universal energy into physical reality.

While cynics sniff at this kind of theory, it's been propounded in a variety of ways by New Age philosophers and quantum physicists. Others, including many First Nations people, don't actually need it. Their cultural philosophy assumes the bird was sent specifically with that message, a natural traveler between worlds.

The Mohawk, for instance, recognize the eagle, the bird that soars highest in the sky, as the one who brings messages to and from the Creator. The Navajo see the mountain bluebird as a great spirit in animal form, associated with the rising sun. The bluebird song reminds Najavos to rise at dawn and greet the sun. It's also performed as a revered song in the winter Nightway ceremony just before sunrise on the final day.

Paula Gunn Allen, a Laguna tribe poet and author, says that conversations between humans and other creatures are natural. In her book *Grandmothers of the Light*, she tells of a conversation between a woman and a chickadee, where the little bird had come specifically to teach the woman about respect for the small creatures of the world. The story isn't told as a metaphor or a psychological construct, or hallucinatory madness. It doesn't require a theoretical context, a psychological explanation, or medication. It's simply part of the normal relationship between human and bird, or human and animal, or human and rock for that matter.

Such conversations, she says,

> inform consciousness and direct awareness within as well as without, and they connect with deep levels of being, not because the figures they tell about are immaterial denizens of the shadowy world of the unconscious, but because the supernaturals live within the same environs that humans occupy, and interchanges with them are necessarily part of the fabric of human experience." (p. 7)

Only Western rationalists need to explain this reality. The wiser course, Allen suggests, is to watch for the opportunity to interact, expect it, and respect it when it occurs, knowing it's part of the natural order of things.

That idea doesn't exist only in the past or in Native American communities. Leslie Nase is a fifty-two-year-old Vermont shaman who communicates with the spirits of deceased animals and birds for their human companions. In that sense, she is herself a kind of human bird, moving between realms. She is also an exotic bird, vividly painted by a kind of birthmark called a port-wine stain. A vibrant purple swath covers one ear and half her tongue, and part of her face and throat, ending at her heart. When she was little, she was told she was painted differently, and that her birthmark was a gift from God.

Raised Congregationalist, she's been doing shamanic work for about ten years for all kinds of people, from local farmers who are sometimes shy about their interest in such things, to writer Jon Katz, known for his books on dogs. She says that when she started, it simply gave her the platform for doing what she always loved. "I've always had animals in my life. I always had a,—well, a 'spirit guide' we call it now, but back then we called it an 'imaginary friend.' I also had a bird in my room—Albert the pigeon. I had a wrought-iron bed and he perched on it. It was the perfect perch, and he stayed there until he was ready to go. It was kind of funny, because I lived in a rural place, but we found each other."

That kind of sentence should be familiar by now.

A bird also figures in the beginning of her shamanistic work. Her first trip to Spirit Hollow to attend a seminar on shamanism was marked by nasty weather and all the details of daily life that make you late for what you really want to do. She arrived at the seminar knowing they'd already started, asking herself what she was doing here, questioning her decision to come. As she hurried across the courtyard, she heard a swishing sound, and looked up to see a huge owl land in a tree above her. "It sat there, just looking at me. I was in awe, the way you are with a bird like that, one you don't often see. And I knew I'd walked into something life changing."

Birds are, she says, simply the best physical form for messengers. Even the spirits need some measure of practicality in dealing with the world, and birds come in the best package for delivering messages, Leslie says. "Their color and their fluttering motion draw your attention. In a split second they can be right in your face, or make a sound with their wings or give a cry so you're aware they're overhead. And they're common enough that anyone can relate to them."

Leslie also believes that connection with birds is healing on a mundane level. Once she took part in a community theater production that used many different birdcalls in the background. A woman who was part of the show knew all the bird calls and told the others what birds they were listening to. "It was wonderful to see her face light up as people in the group asked her to identify the calls. She was really using her sense of hearing, and that creates such perceptual pleasure. We forget how important that kind of thing is, as we get all involved in our heads, in our busy lives."

Shamans aren't the only ones who think so. The most common response I've had when I mentioned this book has been, "Oh, I had a funny bird thing happen once."

One such person was Meg Shipton. She's a tall, lean, attractive woman, with a dancer's body and an enthusiastic, positive outlook. Her work as a movement artist contributes to both the body and the manner. You can easily imagine her swirling scarves, dancing with beauty. You wouldn't easily guess at the hard knocks she's survived.

Probably the worst was the death of her son, born with a congenital heart defect. That kind of grief never fully dissipates, but Meg says a little bird helped her heal it.

On the four-year anniversary of his death, she and her husband and children were on their way home from their annual camping trip in Cape Cod. They'd stopped at a restaurant to eat, and while she was paying up her husband went out to the car with the kids. And outside, dancing around the parking lot, was a small blue parakeet. When Meg came out, the kids called to her excitedly, "Mom—look! Look at the bird!"

"We didn't think we should just leave it," Meg said, "We were going to catch it, but just like that, the bird flew up and landed on my husband's shoulder. And there it stayed."

She made a connection between the event and the anniversary date, seeing it as a gift. The little bird rode home on Meg's finger, where it fell asleep, tucking its beak in its wing, a small visitor to console her for the nestling she couldn't keep.

They named him Moby Dick, and he became one of the family. He never lived in a cage, but had a shelf by the window with food and water. A playful little spirit, he used hang out in their ficus tree in the livingroom, or swing upside down from the chandelier. He was a character—one you couldn't avoid. She came downstairs one day to find all her houseguests wearing hats because Moby was hopping from head to head.

His presence was healing, but the following year brought back the pain. One day the following August, she and her son Schuyler were home alone. Schuyler, at seven, was an impulsive, fiery boy. He was playing on their screened-in porch when Moby landed on the open door between house and porch, and Schuyler started moving the door back and forth to get him to fly. He didn't feel like flying, and Schuyler, in little boy way, thought to himself, "Well, if I slam it he'll fly."

Moby stayed put, and disaster followed. Caught in the slammed door, the little bird died.

"Schuyler was horrified—at himself, at what happened," Meg says. "It was just about as awful as you can imagine. There we were, alone, and what do you do with the rest of the day?"

What they did was weep, and bury the bird. Then they went to a nursery and found a blue ceramic birdbath, blue balloon flowers, and white phlox.

In looking back, Meg says the lesson was one that her son "deeply integrated. You could say that Moby totally offered himself, in every way, shape and form."

Schuyler was two when his baby brother died, and hadn't really been able to process his mother's grief or his own feelings. A strong, supercoordinated high energy child, the death of the bird taught him a hard lesson in impulsivity and consequences. It also allowed both mother and son to more fully process the cycle of grief.

"Having Moby around for that year was like a little more time with the baby I'd lost. And then, what happened, Schuyler really collapsed in grief. He kept wanting to do the moment over. But he learned from it. We all did."

I know from personal experience how painful it is to inadvertently harm a bird. During the year I was writing my novel *These Dreams*, which includes a bird sanctuary based on the Berkshire Bird Paradise, I hit three birds with my car and killed them. I'd never even come close to hitting one before that. When I was writing a bird death scene, a crow somehow got inside my house, flew up my stairs, and crashed into the wall just outside my office, killing itself. Bird deaths plagued the entire novel, right up to the final radio interview for the book. When I left it, the car in front of me hit a robin. He didn't stop, but I did, and my lasting memory of that book experience is kneeling by the side of the road with a dying Robin in my hands.

I'm guessing that the number of bird deaths I experienced that year exceeded any statistical norm, and whether you call it coincidence or synchronicity is up to you. I also wanted to know what a spiritual take on it would be, so I asked Leslie.

She, shaman-like, responded with a question. "What did you learn?" she asked me.

"I learned about fragility," I said. "And impermanence. I learned that just because something is temporary, that doesn't make it less meaningful, or beautiful or powerful or good."

"And did that go into the book?" she asked.

Yes, I told her. It most certainly did. In fact, the novel was very much about that.

"Then you learned what they wanted you to learn," she said.

In the twenty-first century, people believe in the magic of the internet and airplanes and nanobots. Is it possible to also believe that birds bring messages to humans on a regular basis, as part of their nature? In answer, I offer something from the website for the PBS series *The Life of Birds*, which notes that ravens will let other ravens know when a carcass is nearby for feasting on, because it's safer to feast in a group. However, it's believed they also tip off other species, such as wolves, who will rip the carcass open and make the meat more accessible. In Africa, the bird known as the honeyguide lures badgers to bees nests and eat the leftovers. Honeyguides also call and fly back and forth to draw local human attention to the location of honeycombs, and are rewarded with their own share of honey for this service.

Whatever theory of human/bird interaction you ascribe to, it's clear that they often lift our spirits in many ways. The Mohawk, in their central ceremony Words Before All Else, thank everything in nature for what it does. When they thank birds, they say the Creator made them knowing we'd have days when our hearts were on the ground and we wouldn't want to go on. Birdsong and the bright flash of red a cardinal remind us that beauty and joy are still possible after all.

Birds perform their greatest service for us simply by showing up. And once you notice them showing up, they show up more, pointing you where you need to go, in small ways or large.

For Pete Dubacher, they show up every day. But then again, so does he.

FIVE

$\mathcal{P}in\ \mathcal{F}eathers$

The bird with the keenest sense of smell may be the turkey vulture. Sir David Attenborough conducted a remarkable experiment. He buried some meat in leaf litter. Well within an hour, vultures had detected the smell from above the tree canopy and half a mile away, and located the meat.

—*www.pbs.org/lifeofbirds/champions/index.html*

Some birds seem to indulge in "intelligent" play. The kea, a New Zealand parrot, has been filmed ripping (inedible) windscreen wipers off cars. Young keas, in a neat variation of ringing the doorbell and running away, are known to drop rocks on roofs to make people run outside.

Jack the jackdaw was raised by wildlife film producer John Downer. As soon as Jack was mature, he was released into the wild. However, he couldn't stay away. "One thing he is totally fascinated by is telephones," said Downer. "He knows how to hit the loudspeaker button and preset dial button. Once we came into the office to find him squawking down the telephone to the local travel agent."

—*www.pbs.org/lifeofbirds/birdbrains/index.html*

2 P.M., *Berkshire Bird Paradise*
"THE TRICK IS to keep moving," Pete tells me.

It's a trick he's mastered. Right now, he's dragging a hose around from one bird house to the next, seeing who's thirsty, who wants a swim, who needs a bath. I've been following him around for two hours, and I have no idea how he keeps track of his daily rounds. Maintenance tasks include daily water changes, feeding, cleaning, renewing woodchips in some houses and cleaning old bones out of others, sorting produce donations for the emus and the ostrich, checking on nestlings and injuries, giving medicine to those who need it, chopping, stacking, and hauling wood, and more. All of it, for more than a thousand birds.

That, of course, doesn't include the constant building and repair projects, the tours for schools and visitors, talking with donors, keeping up with people who have left birds here and occasionally come to visit, transporting birds to places like the Clark Museum for special programs, working with volunteer students, and, of course, keeping up with the human family who also lives here.

That last is important, because Pete is as meticulous with the humans who are involved with the sanctuary as with the birds. "The two most important words in the language are thank you," he tells me. "I write thank you notes, pick up the phone and call people. What they're doing here matters, and I want to make sure they hear me say that."

When visitors come he takes time with them, showing them around, listening to their concerns if they're leaving a bird with him, just chatting if they're new to the place. Everyone who shows up is potentially a friend and member of the Paradise family, and he treats them as such. That's true whether they leave a donation or not. There's no strict admission fee here, and what any visitor wants to offer is what Pete accepts.

And he keeps moving. That's the trick to running the place.

After he's filled some water bowls, Pete drags out a plastic kiddie swimming pool and hoses it out. "Watch this," he says to me.

Immediately, we're surrounded by little ducks, all honking softly with duck delight. One of them stands on Pete's foot and honks up at him. He smiles. "It doesn't take a lot to make them really happy."

The duck hops off his foot and splashes into the water. It's a wood duck, named Woody, and it arrived here through a twisted circuit of connections, from nature writer Bill Danielson's sister.

Wood ducks nest in trees and when the babies hatch they all bail out and head for water. Frequently, one gets lost along the way, and then wanders up to someone like a character in a book, asking, "Are you my mother?"

But wood ducks are notoriously hard to raise. They'll seem fine and healthy, but they won't eat. Everyone Bill knew was convinced that a wood duck was a dead duck, but his sister made it her mission to save this one. She took Woody to water and observed him pecking around the shore. From this, she tried mincing earthworms and putting them in the shallows. It worked, and Woody thrived.

When he seemed old enough she tried releasing him at a wildlife center, but he kept cozying up the humans, and he wasn't doing well. He'd imprinted on people. So he came back, and became a family member, even attending family parties. He was a guest at a party at Bill's house, and DEC pathologist Ward Stone was also there. He was mesmerized by Woody. "You got one to live? I—I can't believe it!" he kept saying.

Through Ward, they found out about the Berkshire Bird Paradise, and that seemed like a place where Woody could have both human and waterfowl friends. They sent him to his new home, where he continues to thrive.

"I think Pete likes him," Bill told me. "I've got pictures of Woody on his head."

Pete does like him, as he likes all his birds. Even the ones that are, to most people, uninteresting or even ugly. Behind us, in an open aviary, a raven opens its wings and caws. I turn to look and it settles down, preening at its feathers.

"Just wanted attention?" I ask.

"Probably. They're really social birds. That's why I put them all in together."

In the aviary with the raven are two other ravens, a few crows, and some turkey buzzards. I've seen all of them on the wing, and I've seen some ravens and crows pretty close up, but I've only seen the buzzards circling high above, riding sky thermals. Their bright red faces are marked with black rings around the eyes, which gives them the look of sad clowns, or weary professors.

"I didn't realize they had those eye rings," I say. One walks over to inspect me more closely. Its presence is soft and rather apologetic. Scavengers and carrion eaters, one doesn't think of them as pretty birds, but they have a gentle demeanor that surprises me.

"Yeah. I like the buzzards," Pete notes. "They're also really social, and kind of sweet natured. But most places won't take them. They're too common."

After a good long look at me, the buzzard turns its head away and wanders into one of the small play houses within the aviary. This whole aviary looks kind of like a small, enclosed daycare center. In one corner there's a colorful plastic child-sized playhouse, and at the center there's a thick rope hung with bells and colorful balls. The birds move through their small kingdom with apparent contentment. One of the ravens crawls over the ropes, picking at them and cawing under his breath.

"The buzzards like caves, so the playhouse gives them a place to tuck away," Pete says. And the rest is for the ravens and crows. They're really smart birds, and they like to pick at ropes and things. Keeps them occupied, and that keeps them from getting anxious, picking at each other or themselves."

"Kind of like kids," I say.

"Or like us."

Pete peers inside the aviary, and focuses on one of the smaller crows. "That guy doesn't look so good. Hang on a minute."

He goes inside and moves to a crow who looks morose, sitting on the floor away from the others. He picks it up and talks to it softly. "You okay buddy? Need a little time out?"

"What's wrong?" I ask.

"I don't know. Could be nothing. Maybe stress. Birds get stressed pretty easy."

As he holds it, a raven approaches and caws up at him. It pecks at his foot, picks up a woodchip and drops it on his shoe, then looks up at him inquiringly. He looks down at it. "Yeah, I see you," he says. "We're not playing right now." Then, to me, "Ravens are curious about everything."

He takes the crow and leaves, and I follow him to where the tropical birds are housed. There's a shelf of cat carriers across from the cages, and he pops the crow into one, with a bowl of water and a little food. This is the time out place, a bird retreat in cat carrier motels. I suppose there's a certain justice to that.

"You think this'll help?" I ask.

He shrugs. "We'll see. I'll keep checking on him, make sure there's no infection or anything. But a lot of times, all they need is a little rest and quiet and whatever's bothering them goes away," he says. "Sometimes the best thing you can do for them is just leave them alone."

"And if there's a problem?"

"I've got the basics to take care of problems here. I usually do my own vet work. There's not really anyone close enough that I can get to around here who deals with birds. Not too many vets in general who deal with wild birds or animals. There's no profit in it," he says. "Sometimes they send birds to me. One vet called because he found a heron with a dangling leg, and he wasn't sure what to do."

"How'd you learn?"

"The usual. I read, I pay attention. And I call Ward Stone when I'm baffled. He taught me a lot."

I realize that I've never heard Pete talk about birds dying. With so many, he must have to go through that, and I don't know how he manages to deal with it. Is it a numbers thing? Like nurses or doctors, you simply adjust to a certain rate of attrition. I ask about it, and he gives me a bewildered look.

"Well, actually I don't get many that die," he says. "I mean, there's a natural mortality rate when they get old, but it's pretty low other than that. They usually just live out their lives here, and stay healthy."

I think of birds as fragile, but Pete says otherwise. "Birds are actually pretty tough. The old saying, an ounce of prevention is worth a pound of cure, and the one that says you are what you eat—I follow those two. I'm big on good nutrition. If you feed them properly and keep their water and space clean, they'll be very healthy unless they have a hidden ailment. I'd rather feed them more than not enough. And make sure they have plenty of room for exercise."

Occasionally, he says, a wild hawk or owl might fly in and take out a duck. Sometimes the birds fight during breeding season and he has to separate the more aggressive ones, put them in time-out. And last year someone brought him an owl that was hit by a car, one he thought wouldn't make it.

"The face was a bloody mess," Pete remembers. "I told the people if this owl lives an hour it'll be a miracle. But we took care of him, and now he's back out in the wild."

I sigh. Birdwatcher Rich Guthrie told me that in the wild birds about sixty percent never even make it out of the nest. Pete is the bird whisperer.

With the crow tucked away for a little R&R, we emerge into daylight again.

"Hey—did you see all the new owls?" Pete asks. "They're from when the Raptor Center in Duchess County closed down. Something like fifty birds—hawks, owls, falcons. They asked if I'd take them."

The Raptor Center was founded by Dona Tracy more than twenty-five years ago to house and rehab injured raptors. Its ninety acres was home to about one hundred birds of prey, but financial difficulties forced it to close in 2008. This leaves the Berkshire Bird Sanctuary as the only game in town, the last large-scale facility for injured birds that need long-term or, more often, permanent housing.

"That's a lot to manage, isn't it?" I ask.

"Yeah," he agrees. "But they'd be euthanized if I didn't take them. They're all human-raised, and can't function in the wild."

I follow Pete's rapid strides over to the aviary that houses the owls. Barred owls, Pete tells me. There's a clutch of them, more than half a dozen, perched on roosts, dozing. One opens an eye and waits to see what will happen next. When nothing does, he goes back to sleep.

"They seem content," I say.

"Oh yeah. At night they get talkative, though. You'll have to come out and hear them."

"What would happen if you just let them go?" I ask.

"They'd starve. Or they'd be picked off pretty quick. Great horned owls would get them."

"Owls eat—other owls?"

"Yeah. These ones eat spotted owls. In fact, they're a problem that way. It's one reason why no one really cares about them much, I suppose. Anyway, they're home now."

They look it. Fluffing feathers, bunching themselves up into fuzzy footballs, they close their eyes and return to their owl dreams. Next door, in a large cage by itself there's another owl, and this one bangs around, flying from perch to the wire frame of the cage. Pete goes over to it. "This one's wild. Got in a tangle with a skunk. I wasn't sure he was gonna make it, but he's almost ready to go back out."

I remember this one. I was here the day he was brought in. I pulled in the driveway only to see Pete with a large owl tucked under his arm, in conversation with a couple who were getting ready to leave in their pick-up truck. Pete is the bird go-to guy for many people besides me. The wild ones are released as soon as they're healed, but sixty percent of the birds are here for life, and raptors can live for decades. Caring for such birds marked Pete's transition to this work being a lifelong commitment.

"When I got my first eagle, I knew I was in it for good," he says. "That was kind of a fluke, really."

Since the whole place is a kind of fluke, that's no surprise. What happened was that in 1989 a woman called from a zoo in Indiana. She had a bald eagle about to be euthanized if Pete couldn't take it. But keeping eagles requires a federal license, which he didn't have. He knew how long it could take to get one, and in the meantime, the eagle would be dead of red tape.

Fortunately, a friend of Pete's, Bob Kaufmann, stopped by. He lived in Massachusetts, and happened to be neighbor with Tom Jorling, who was then commissioner of New York State Department of Environmental Conservation (DEC). Pete told Bob the problem, and Bob contacted Jorling immediately. No more than 2 hours later Pete got a call from Margurite Donnelly, of the Federal Fish and Wildlife Service. She asked for the phone number of the Indiana zoo. An hour later she called Pete again and told him the eagle would be his in a couple of days.

"It was almost like a person on death row," Pete recalls. "They got him a stay of execution, and then a full pardon."

Pete, on the other hand, now had a life sentence. He was aware that if he walked away, the birds would have to be euthanized, and he wouldn't let that happen.

He quit cooking, and wasn't sorry to leave that profession. "In cooking, you're only as good as your last meal, and people forget about that pretty quickly," he says.

It was more rewarding and, in spite of the workload, more relaxing to work with the birds. For him, they provided a lasting sense of worth.

In 1989, the sanctuary was also pushed in a new direction, through the unlikely auspices of the IRS. In that year, Pete received notice that they wanted to audit him. At the time he was running the sanctuary as a small business, and they had quite a few questions about his expenditures.

"My father told me to just bring my stuff and show them and don't worry about it, but I was scared to death," Pete says.

He went in ready to do battle, thinking at least he'd go down fighting. When he sat down with the woman, she opened her book, looked at him and said, "Why do you have rose bushes as an expense? You've got all these birds, and you're deducting roses?"

He was perplexed, he admits. All that worry, and they're only asking about his roses? That's an audit? He explained that he was making the place nice for the birds, and the people who came to see them. He didn't want it to be a dump, after all. And the birds need plants around them, too.

The auditor was still confused. She said, "Look, we audited you because you deduct almost all your pay for the birds. We just couldn't believe it."

When it turned out to be clearly true, all Pete's money went to the birds, she said, "Why are you doing this? You should be a nonprofit. Then you can write grants and accept donations."

That was a new concept for Pete, not one he'd thought of at all, and he had no idea how it worked. The auditor gave him the names of people to contact for help with setting it up, She gave him the people to contact for nonprofit status and talked him through the beginning of that process. By 1990, the Berkshire Bird Paradise was a 501(c)3, well on its way to becoming a lasting haven for Pete and his birds.

The IRS story is typical of the bird sanctuary, which seems to be watched over by angels who appear in the form of DEC commissioners and IRS auditors. Pete's life combines Jungian synchronicity and plain good luck with lots of hard work to create a place that sometimes seems to exist on a metaphoric high plain. Between feedings and cleanings, paying the bills and repairing smashed owl faces, there's a great deal of beauty here, and that matches bird life, which is both precarious and tough, existing for forty million years on an equal mix of gritty grubbing for carrion and seed, and an inherent miraculous beauty.

Birds are creatures that both inspire art and *are* art by nature of their being. How they do that, and what that means to us, is what we'll look at next.

SIX

Making Beauty

Vaughan Williams's orchestral romance, *The Lark Ascending*, was inspired not only by English folk themes but by George Meredith's poem of the same title. Included on the flyleaf of the published work were the following lines from Meredith's poem:

> He rises and begins to round,
> He drops the silver chain of sound,
> Of many links without a break,
> In chirrup, whistle, slur and shake.
> For singing till his heaven fills,
> 'Tis love of earth that he instils,
> And ever winging up and up,
> Our valley is his golden cup
> And he the wine which overflows
> to lift us with him as he goes.
> Till lost on his aerial rings
> In light,
> and then the fancy sings.

I ONCE HAD a discussion in a college class about the difference between humans and animals. What behavior of ours separated us from nonhuman species? Was it using tools?

No, because animals—including birds—have been observed not only using but making tools. The woodpecker finch of the Galapagos trims twigs to use for prying insects from bark, and a captive cactus finch learned to do the same thing after watching his wild cousin from his cage. The woodpecker finch, like a good teacher, helped by passing a twig he'd already prepared through the cage as a kind of model.

That kind of example also shows that we aren't the only creatures who possess intelligence beyond mere genetically programmed instinct. Other birds also demonstrate this. In Japan, ravens were observed perching in nut trees near crosswalks on city streets. They toss nuts into the road, and wait for cars to run them over and crush the shell. Then, they wait patiently until the light turns red and traffic stops before they hop down into the road to retrieve their nuts. When the light changes and traffic starts to move, they fly back to their perches. Since they didn't start doing this until 1990, they're clearly still learning new behaviors, suited to their environments.

Birds even lie, pretending to be injured in order to draw predators away from their nest, so we can't lay claim to that trait exclusively. Then the difference between us and birds must be the use of symbolism, the making of art, which seems restricted to humans. Hmm. Maybe, and maybe not.

Birds are chivalrous creatures, as a rule, and their courtship rituals often seem, well, highly symbolic. The grebe and his mate dance on the water in intricate synchronization of each other's movements. Hawks dance in the sky, circling and calling to each other as they ascend higher and higher. Eagles also sky dance with potential mates, sometimes ending the dance by clasping talons and spinning in free-fall to the earth, letting go only at the last possible moment necessary to achieve a safe landing. Or, as sometimes happens, not letting go at all and crashing to earth still clutching each other.

And then, there's the vogelkopf bower bird, an unrivaled architect of love's art. These birds, native to Australia and New Guinea, spend weeks building small bowers out of grasses, in varying shapes and sizes, that look like something a little girl would construct for a family of fairies. The thatched roofs and sides are supported by sticks used for framing and grounding, a rather intricate structural creation. When that's done, the bower bird starts decorating.

He gathers flowers, fruits, seeds, and arranges them meticulously in and around the bower. A pile of dark, shining insect shells will be offset by bright pink flower blossoms. A mound of smooth round pebbles create contrast with a grouping of golden leaves. These items are not just flung about, either. The bower bird spends days making sure everything is exactly where he wants it, adding, deleting, or shifting items with no less care than a writer spends over the arrangement of words on a page. Each bower is unique to the builder. And none of them are used as nests.

They're display houses, avian loveshacks for the consummation of desire. When a female hears the male's song and finds the loveshack good, they have their moment, and then the female goes off alone to build her nest and raise her young. The male bower bird continues singing, waiting for his next visitor.

Science often dismisses such efforts by saying they're "just" genetically programmed behaviors. But genetics are themselves an astonishment and a wonder, for one thing. For another, no matter what part genetics play, each bird still creates something unique and beautiful. In the same way, you could say that we may be genetically programmed to court and spark, but how each of us chooses to do so is unique. The red Corvette is, perhaps, just a loveshack of a different name. Nor is the behavior of the man who parades it around that different from the bower bird's.

This similarity of behavior makes visible our kinship as creatures sharing not only a planet, but also interests that are not, after all, so different. Of course, human courting can be viewed as simply instinctive, but that doesn't diminish its highly individualized style in birds or humans. Both species choose their own way to create attraction, and in the process make beauty of one kind or another. And both species apparently find that important.

Darwin, in *The Descent of Man*, points out that birds wouldn't have developed beautiful feathers and songs if the female bird didn't appreciate them. The bower bird, which is drab, substitutes elaborate love shacks for brilliant plumage. How many humans do the same?

We seem to share a similar appreciation of beauty, and perhaps we even learned ours from them since they were here first.

Early humans must have absorbed bird colors and markings, bird song and bird grace in flight into our own deepest sense of what's beautiful. And we've made use of what we've learned ever since. Wearing feathers as capes and headdresses may be as old as humanity. Ancient Mayans had a specific job listing for feather workers, and the feather capes of Hawaiian leaders were magnificent to behold. Though that kind of use of feathers is most often associated with indigenous cultures, Europeans were no slouches. In 1898, Great Britain imported twenty-five million wild birds for use in fashion and millinery.

Birds have inspired human creativity in dance as well as fashion. Stravinsky's *Firebird* and Tchaikovsky's *Swan Lake* are just two ballets where birds make their appearance. In an art that often seeks to defy gravity, or at least play with its limits, birds frequently serve as inspiration. But perhaps the most obvious art where birds have instructed us is music.

We love birdsong as much as we love bird's capacity for flight. Where I live, just at the end of winter, the red-winged blackbirds return in large flocks and fill the surrounding woods. The first year we moved here, on a day when the sun was shining but soft fat snowflakes were falling all around, I came home to a chorus of silver-throated singing that emanated from the woods like the music of distant fairy folk. The sound was layered and complex, with trilling, soft raspings, and an impossible bell-like clarity shining through.

Nature writer Bill Danielson tells me they do this singing to distinguish their group from other birds who are returning at the same time. Like many bird vocalizations, it has a specific purpose, and a recognizable pattern. Alarm calls, for instance, are high-pitched, and short, to serve the purpose of warning that a predator is nearby.

But singing, different than simple birdcall, is learned, and often specific to a region as well as a species, so that blue jays may have one song in one neighborhood, and another somewhere else. Sometimes songs are sung to attract a mate, or define territory, but they're also sung outside of mating season, without territoriality. Sometimes birds just sing, and ornithologists still don't know why that's so, since singing takes energy, and is often risky because it alerts predators to a possible meal. Still, birds sing. A lot.

During breeding season, nightingales don't eat at night. They only sing, and this even at the risk of attracting nighthawks who might eat them. Like all birds, they can sing incredibly complex songs, partly because their more complex vocal structure enables them to sing more than one note at a time. And according to PBS's *Life of Birds*, the superb lyrebird of Australia uses that equipment to mimic just about anything it hears, from the human voice, to the sound of a chainsaw or a camera shutter, one sound after the other spilling from its throat without a break.

Again, we can chalk all of that singing up to instinct, or we can speculate about the artistic nature of birds, as Darwin did. We can also simply enjoy the gift—or do as musician David Rothenberg did and play along.

As he describes in his book, *The Mystery of Birdsong*, Rothenberg spent time at the National Aviary in Pittsburgh, in the year 2000, jamming with the birds. They sang, and he played along with them. He played, and they listened to him and responded, and he listened to them and responded, and together, they made beautiful music. It was, for him, a life-changing experience. He wondered if birds have wanted just this kind of interaction, one where we play with them and learn from them as friends rather than studying them like specimens. Rothenberg says, "Playing with birds rather than merely thinking about birds, I began to feel what it is like to be a bird. I do not look for proof, but only possibility, and hope for new ways to interact" (p. x).

The Mystery of Birdsong goes on to explore the different ways that both science and art have dealt with birdsong. Rothenberg ultimately prefers living the mystery, saying, "Can any explanation for beauty be satisfactory? Despite all we have uncovered about how evoution is able to produce marvelous bird songs through generations of slow transformation, no knowledge tempers our joy. . . . Information does not really touch experience" (p. xi).

Like birds, and perhaps because of their tutelage, we are drawn to displays of singing and dancing. The serenading male, the woman who can belt the blues or woo us with fluted high notes—that's sexy. Singing provides an expression of the heart that we resonate with emotionally, even if we can't make the notes ourselves. We are connected to birds emotionally through song, and no amount of science can or should change that.

Though I find it interesting to know why birds sing and what their songs signify, I'm even more intrigued by the question of what in our being is similar to theirs, that we both share this appreciation of beautiful and joyful noises, even when it doesn't get us food or mates. Musicians have been known to keep making their songs in spite of poverty and rejection, physical hardship or disability. And quite a few of them were instructed in songmaking by birds.

Beethoven, not so different from our avian friends, used the song of the nightingale (flute), the cuckoo (clarinet), and the quail (oboe) for his Sixth Symphony, the Pastoral. My brother Stanley, a violinist and composer, tells me Beethoven also used the call of the yellow hammer bird as the basis for the opening phrase of his Fifth Symphony. Right now, if you go to youtube.com and do a search of Beethoven, you'll find a video of someone who has taught their parrot to sing the opening of Beethoven's Fifth Symphony, bringing the song full circle back to the birds.

Beethoven is joined by many others whose music was inspired by birds. When I'm writing a book, I make a playlist of songs to listen to while I'm writing, a different list for each book. The one for this book is eclectic, and includes the Beatles ("Blackbird"), Kim and Reggie Harris ("I Have a Million Nightingales?"), Vaughn Williams (*The Lark Ascending*), Magpie ("Isle of May," which is about Puffins), and many more. My brother has promised to send me a CD of a piece he's written that has a bobolink call in it, based on an Emily Dickinson poem ("Some Keep the Sabbath"). There's more than enough bird-inspired musical material to make my playlist possibilities seem infinite.

Birds make art, and inspire art, and are in themselves artful. We can spend time figuring out what purpose this serves and how it happens. Or we can ask ourselves a more answerable question, which is why we love it so. And the answer to that will probably be as varied as the people it comes from.

My son's reason was one I particularly liked. He said, "I think I appreciate birds best at the times when I can't see them, but I can hear them. You know they're around somewhere, but all you have is their voices. Then, it's like angels are watching all around."

Yes. It certainly is. But birds, like all artists, must eat. Pete knows this, and makes sure to keep his birds well fed.

SEVEN

$\mathcal{F}eeding$

When the little bird finished singing, the Miller looked up at him. "Why, that was a beautiful song," he said. "Sing it again!"

"I only sing for free once," the bird replied. "If you want to hear it again, you'll have to pay me."

—*From the folktale "The Juniper Tree"*

3 P.M., Berkshire Bird Paradise

"RATS," I NOTE.

"Yeah," Pete agrees.

The sky is beginning to cloud, and the sun is rolling down toward the west as he uncovers a pile of dead and frozen rats. White rats. A wheelbarrow full of frozen dinners.

"Where do they come from?"

"A cosmetic lab. They're the best-fed rats you can get."

"The birds don't mind that they're—um—dead?" I ask.

"They don't seem to."

While I mull the political ramifications of using dead rats from cosmetic labs to feed birds in a sanctuary, Pete picks through the bodies, transfers a bunch to another wheelbarrow, and we begin rolling them toward the eagle residences.

He spent a long time figuring out how to build these, based on what eagles need in general, and on the individual disabilities his eagles have. Some, wingless or blind, live in large, low wire-enclosed aviaries made of wood, with an open area and back-room privacy, and plenty of perches made from tree branches.

Others live in nesting aeries, wooden structures that look like giant tree houses without the tree, towering about fifty feet high. We duck into one of these, and stand in a kind of ante-room area with a lower ceiling. From an opening at the other end, I can see the branches that provide perches for the eagles. One of them is hopping around on them, waiting for lunch, aware that Peter's presence signals its imminent arrival. Pete leans over and tosses in a rat.

Immediately the eagle falls on it and starts ripping. Pete tosses in a few more. "They're hungry," he notes.

I look around, see the bones of many lunches at my feet. Rats, roadkill, a mingling of menus. Birds move easily between realms. Earth and sky, sublime and grotesque, dance and destruction. Pick a dichotomy, and they traverse it.

"Y'know, when Betty Ann came here, the first thing I had her do was clean out the cages," Pete says, smiling wryly.

I think about the bower bird, and wonder at human mating rituals. "And she kept coming back?"

"She did. I tell you, I was surprised. I was forty-five. I figured I'd be single the rest of my life. It's like some things are just meant to be, right?"

Looking at Betty Ann you wouldn't think she was the type to take on marriage to a man who fed dead rats to birds. Her hair and make-up are always impeccable, her bright blue eyes and auburn hair making her look younger than her fifty-some years. She seems more like a woman who shops at Bloomingdales than one who lives with more than a thousand birds, married to the man who takes care of them. But their courtship happened, like so many important events at the sanctuary, by mysterious misadventure.

Betty Ann and her siblings were raised in Pittsfield, Massachusetts, by a single mother, because when their father came back from the Korean War he was too damaged to be a parent to them. She was apparently as tough and energetic as Betty Ann, and would tell her, "When you feel at your worst, that's when you get out your best lipstick and put the mascara on, and go out there looking good."

Her family was in the restaurant business, and after growing up with the never-ending work and stress that went with that, Betty

Ann wanted something different. So she went to Russell Sage College in Troy to study physical therapy, earning her degree in 1982, at the age of forty. Right after her graduation she took a drive out to Grafton Lake. She wanted to be by herself, consider her options for what she'd do next. She was so deep in thought she missed the turn-off, drove past the lake, and then took a wrong turn—which landed her at the Berkshire Bird Paradise.

She was, like many people who visit, enchanted. She'd never seen anything like it before. She went back to volunteer her time, and just as Pete said, the first task he handed her was cage cleaning.

"It was the owls," she tells me. "He shows me this bird cage and says, 'Here, clean this.' It's filled with bones and dead things, right? I think he figured that'd get rid of me. Instead, for some reason, I thought to myself, 'I'm gonna marry him.' I don't even know why I thought that. I'd lived on my own forever and I figured I always would. I was going to go to the Carolinas and work. But then, I kept coming back."

She started bringing medicinal oils that she makes for the birds, and one day, when she was putting them on the cranes, she asked him, "Are you seeing anyone."

He said, "No, but I'm interested in you."

You could say their courtship is the direct opposite of the bower bird, but if you look at from another angle, there are actually some startling similarities. Consider that the Berkshire Bird Paradise is Pete's bower. And consider that Betty Ann saw in his architecture a fundamental display of his character.

"It was his kindness that drew me," she told me. "The way he cares for the birds. The attention he gives them. A man like that, you have to know he's something special."

The best part of being here, for her, is the quiet. "I go into the city and I can't stand the noise, the city traffic, all the agitation. You see people with two TVs on at once, the radio going, or people walking down the street all plugged in to something. It amazes me. I don't know how they do it. I need a little quiet for my soul."

Pete and Betty Ann have been married for fifteen years now, and both of them work together with the birds, but they each remain independent as well. She works at a Hoosick Falls health center, in a place that's community run. She says that she and her daughter go out when they want, and she's learned to take care of herself even while she's helping Pete with the birds and with his parents.

"Winter can be really hard here. Breaking trails through the snow when all the birds still need to be fed. A lot of times we can't get out because we're not a priority in terms of plowing. There's lots of hard work, and isolation. People who move here from the city often don't last much beyond their first winter. They run out of water, have problems with the electricity, and they can't take it."

She says she was particularly lonely when she first moved in, but then she was invited to a quilting party. "I said I don't know how to sew, but that didn't matter. The neighbors saw me with my hair and make-up, out here working like a man, and then I was in."

Besides winter, the hardest part is when she worries about money. Then, Pete tells her, "Don't worry. Our job is to take care of the birds. The rest will take care of itself."

So far, he's been right.

"The birds own this place, not the people," she says. "They're in charge."

The eagle we're feeding stops for a moment, half a dead rat hanging out of its mouth. Briefly, but intently, it turns and stares at me. Like any raptor, the stare of an eagle is intense, their visual capacities far exceeding ours.

I'm reminded of a morning that I went to the University at Albany campus to teach a class. As I clipped across the podium toward the humanities building, I saw a red-tailed hawk standing right on the edge of the podium, scanning the field below. I stopped, stared. Other people walked by, but no one else seemed to notice the hawk. I approached, slowly and quietly. The hawk didn't move. I walked closer, and still it didn't move. Finally, I stood next to it, no more than two feet away, at its side.

I tried to see what the hawk saw, and could not. I turned and looked down at it, and it swiveled its head around and looked at me.

For a moment, we stared at each other, two creatures sharing common ground, sharing time and presence. Her golden eyes took me in, determining quickly that I was neither prey nor competition. All knowledge for her came from that sharp, intense gaze, just as all knowledge for my dog comes from sniffing the ground.

Her glance silenced words, made them unnecessary. It was enough to simply be present with each other. Then she lifted her wings and swooped down on the lawn, coming up with a mouse in her beak.

Birds of prey are silent but intense watchers. They stare until they've learned what they need to know, then they turn back to their own lives. At Pete's sanctuary, as the eagle pierced me with his silent gaze, I realized that that's part of what we value in them. We poor humans need words to mediate experience. For raptors, vision is enough. We get a taste of that when they turn their eyes our way.

In pursuit of that experience some people go far. But more often than not, they're the watchers rather than the watched.

 EIGHT

Watching Birds

> I consider myself to have been the bridge between the shotgun and the binoculars in bird watching. Before I came along, the primary way to observe birds was to shoot them and stuff them.
>
> —*Roger Tory Peterson*

PROFESSOR JOHN PIPKIN is a tall, lean drink of water, with a British accent. He teaches in the Geography and Planning Department at the University at Albany, regularly conducts Albany architecture walks, and in his spare time is an avid bird watcher.

"Why?" I ask him, when we meet at the University at Albany's Patroon Room for lunch.

"Well, when I came to this country, I didn't know the wildlife. And we have different birds in England. You see something like an oriole, it makes a big impression. You want to follow up."

John may have seen birdwatching as a way to get acquainted with a new landscape, but the U.S. Fish and Wildlife Service says that around 51.3 million people list birdwatching as an activity, and the industry puts an estimated two billion dollars in the economy. That's a good chunk of cash, spent by a lot of people, most of whom were not born and raised in England. John says it's popular because it satisfies our atavistic need for hunting in a civilized world.

"Birdwatching isn't just peeking out at the visitors to your backyard feeder. It's more like a quest, or a treasure hunt," he tells me. "There's definitely a hunting aspect to it. Hunting without the gun. You're seeking the rare, the unusual. I knew I was a real birder when I braved mosquitoes thick as a shirt in the everglades to put a roseate spoonbill on my list."

Fortunately, you don't have to go that far to indulge in bird-watching. John's collected some fine sightings at places like Five Rivers Environmental Education Center in Delmar, Montezuma National Wildlife Refuge near the Finger Lakes, and the Pine Bush Preserve in Albany.

And, of course, there's always the city dump.

"The dump?" I ask.

"It's a great place if you're collecting gulls," he says. "You'll see lots of different kinds there. And turkey vultures love it. I had quite a moment with a flock of them at the dump. I came upon them unexpectedly, and then I had to back off carefully."

"Um—why? They're not vicious, are they?"

"Oh no, but when they're scared, they throw up on you. I think it's to lighten their load, so they can fly away more quickly. I didn't want a lot of vulture puke on me, as you can imagine."

Who knew that vulture puke was a birding hazard? With dangers like that, I ask him, what is the point of birdwatching? What's the pleasure of it?

For some people, he says, it's a matter of completing their life list, something birdwatchers keep seriously, adding new birds, going places where they can see what they've never seen before. For other people, it's just nice to get out.

"It's a good excuse to be outdoors. You have a goal, but mean-time, you have to sit quietly in nature and just be. You sit still, and the birds come to you. Very zen. And really, watching is a misnomer, because we're listening as well."

The auditory nature of birdwatching is, he says, crucial. You sit and listen, and at first you'll hear only familiar calls. Over time, you'll filter those out, and begin to hear the more exotic calls within them.

John prefers what he calls transitional zones—the places between forest and road, swamp and forest, water and meadow. Here, you'll come across the widest variety of birds as they tra-verse from one land area to another. In such zones, he's seen a scarlet tanager, an Indigo bunting, and a rare vireo all in one sitting.

Then, sometimes, you can try too hard and miss what's ready to leap out at you. Once, he'd been beating around Five Rivers for some time with no luck. He went back to the welcome center, exhausted and disgruntled. There he ran into fellow bird-watcher Ken Able and complained to him, "I haven't seen anything. You?"

"Yeah," Ken said. "A red crossbill."

"Oh God," John said. "Where?"

"Right there," Ken said, and pointed out the window, at the tree in back of the building.

John shrugs at the memory. "As Picasso said, you don't search. You find. Or are found."

Getting birds for your list is one aspect of this recreational activity, but birdwatchers are more than eccentric list fanatics. Their work serves a useful purpose for conservationists and wildlife managers. The New York State Breeding Bird Atlas enlists birdwatchers, who are each responsible for scanning their area and providing proof of the birds that live or build nests there.

"Proof," says John, "is a baby in a nest."

They also keep track of which birds show up in their area in a given time, and all of this provides important information about what birds are doing in the state. It's a sort of census-taking for the birds.

When I asked him what was new in the birdwatching world these days, he said, "Actually, the internet. It's totally changed the scene, made it much more accessible. Getting information about a special sighting used to take some doing. Now there's hotlines, and you can know instantly when something good is spotted. When the European Ruff showed up—a kind of sandpiper with a collar that sticks out like something from Jurassic Park—the crowds were so thick you had to fight to see it."

John enjoys his birdwatching time, but he's not a romantic about it, or a sentimentalist. It seems that for him the birds create the connection with the natural world, maybe even more than to the birds themselves. Even there, he's a realist.

"If anything, getting out in nature reminds you that wildlife is a vast holocaust," he says. "Everything's eating everything else. I had a nuthatch at my feeder once, and along came this cat. It leapt up and grabbed the feeder with one paw, and the bird with the other. Predation at its best."

John has seen, as I have in my back yard, a sharp-shinned hawk feasting on starlings. He's also seen, as I have not, the loggerhead shrike, which catches grasshoppers and sticks them on the thorns of thornbushes to save for later. It can become a kind of massive avian butcher shop, over time.

And backyard birdfeeders, he says, only brings the massacre into the human world. "The birdfeeding industry—think about it. It relies on our hunger for nature, encouraging the visual consumption of birds at feeders. But they only really encourage the junk birds. The ones that are already proliferating, like sparrows and starlings. It gives them a comparative advantage. And, of course, for the neighborhood cats, birdfeeders are like a kind of all-you-can-eat buffet. So that industry commodifies the holocaust of nature."

I'm glad to talk with someone who recognizes the darker side of the natural world but still values the connection with it, on its own terms. Wild is wild, and perhaps all aspects of it are exciting to humans, who are stuck with logical minds and the accoutrements of civilization.

"John," I say to him, "I can always count on you for the cynical point of view. So what do you think of what Pete Dubacher does? Is that going against nature? Defying the holocaust?"

At this, he turns serious. "Oh, no. He's a saint. I don't know how he manages."

That, from my favorite cynic. But I get his point about birdfeeding. We want to be in touch with nature, and that desire can be bought and sold to most of suburban America. Is that good? Bad? Both? Feeding stations encourage birds to lay more eggs, so in that sense, we could be making as many new birds as our cats can kill. Why do I trudge out in the snow when the chickadees scold me that their special sunflower-seed feeder is empty? Why do I make a mess in my kitchen concocting mixtures of rendered suet, seed, berries, and peanut butter? Why does my husband continue to bring home giant bags of nijer seed, mixed seed, sun-flower seeds, even while he complains about the cost?

Because in the deepest part of winter, everything is white and grey except for the cardinal who hops on the branches of our crabapple tree, and that sudden bit of color is beautiful. Or maybe because of the sense of companionship that comes from a tree full of chickadees, juncos, and little woodpeckers.

Personally, I could chalk it up to my own genetic imperative. I come from an Italian family. If something looks hungry, I have to feed it. I'll continue to put out suet, berries, mealworms, and seed, along with about sixty-five million other U.S, citizens, especially in the winter, when the feeding frenzy can be intense.

Birding expert Rich Guthrie says bird feeding is "a harmless selfish activity. There's probably nothing we can do that makes a difference to them. They've survived a long time without us. And one cardinal surviving isn't a long-term issue, but a kid learning to love a cardinal—that's another thing. That's the value of a birdfeeder."

He started birding the way many people I spoke with did—because a parent or a grandparent, an aunt or uncle, introduced them to it. His father was an attorney in New York City, and he would sit outside the office with his cronies and watch the birds. They'd go off on bird sighting adventures in Central Park, or on Staten Island, which was rural then.

"Then, one day I was in the Botanical Gardens in Brooklyn, bringing in insects who were bothering our tree. I came upon three ladies oohing and aahing over something in the shrubs. They didn't know what it was. I told them, 'It's a towhee,' and they were so impressed. I was just a kid, but suddenly I knew something. That was it for me. Coming from a big family, that kind of attention isn't easy to get. I'd found my niche."

Birding is his avocation rather than his career. He's a retired bureaucrat, finally out doing what he loves best, which is study-ing birds, guiding birding tours, sharing his experience of birds with others. He recommends it as a hobby rather than a job, for economic reasons and because he's seen a lot of professionals who get jaded, or get stuck in their little niche and lose touch. They forget the simple things—the beauty of cardinals. Or they look down their noses at the amateurs, who actually provide some important services for the professionals.

"I run into so many people who were exposed to bird life when they were young, and never let go of it. They didn't go anywhere with it as a career, but they didn't let go. And it brings good things in unexpected ways. For one thing, birds connect you to the world. Most of them migrate, so if you're interested in a bird that goes to Mexico or South America, then you get interested in what's happening in those other places as well. Birdwatching encourages global thinking."

The people he takes out on bird walks connect to birds differently than to other creatures. Their color, their beauty, and their ability to fly creates that difference, he believes. They go away—up into the heavens—and then, they come back. That makes us think about our passage between worlds.

"People extend many human attributes out from themselves to the birds. Romance, spiritual yearnings, all that. Maybe it's all imaginary, but it's good anyway. It enlarges our thoughts, our souls."

Rich's connection to birds includes that, he says, but then, he'll put on his science hat, and study them in different ways. He goes out every year as a compiler for the Christmas Bird Count, an event started by the Audobon Society as a counter-tradition to the Christmas hunt. From December 14th to January 5th, tens of thousands of volunteers go out with binoculars and notepads, scouring their assigned areas to count birds, and report back on their sightings. They go out in groups of two or more and drive around, stopping at different points to take numbers.

"It's different from birdwatching," Rich says. "If you're doing a census and you see a warbler, you can't stop and watch. You see a group of gulls, try to identify each kind and how many, jot it down and move on. Then we all go back and sit in a restaurant with other groups and feed numbers to a compiler, who sends the info on to Audobon. "

The data they gather helps researchers and conservationists to study the long-term status of bird populations, informing strategies for protecting birds and their habitats and helping to identify environmental issues that have human as well as avian implications. Rich says it's also a lot of fun.

The local group has grown over the years and now includes the entire ornithology faculty at the University at Albany. It's a jovial, social event, a chance for bird people to do their own flocking. "It's also competitive," Rich notes. "Who got what? Who poached what from where? It's kind of a game, but it's the game that keeps it alive. You give people numerical homework— good luck to you. But put them in a numerical footrace and you'll see them shine."

The rise and fall of the house finch is recorded in their numbers, along with the rise of the bald eagle and disappearance of the ruffed grouse. For the fiftieth annual Catskill bird count, he's working with a statistician to create an illustrative analysis of this data, to tell the story of the numbers they gather. In it they'll try to discern why the meadowlark is less represented, and what's happened to some of the gulls.

Rich is also a licensed bird bander who volunteers with the U.S. Fish and Wildlife Service. Once he puts a serially numbered band on a bird's leg and lets it go, the bird's behavior, its activities, its dangers and preferences, can be tracked. His bird activities earned him a special assignment, and let him add a bird to his list that few can claim. A few years ago, he got a call from Cornell to help with their search in Arkansas for the Ivory Bill woodpecker. On Tuesday of the second week into the search, while he was trudging through swamp, he stopped at some high ground to look at his compass. He looked up, and saw the bird. It was a clear view of the bird, but he couldn't get to his camera, so he missed the shot, but he keeps the moment. And it goes on his list.

"Oh, yes," he tells me, "I'm a lister. It's a competitive thing. Lists take on all kinds of twists, too."

People keep yard lists, county lists, world lists, life lists, and some are ready to hop up at a moments notice when they get word of a rare sighting they want to add to their list. He tells me, "I have a friend who added a whole new category—the sunroof list. And he's got a good one, too."

He agrees with what John Pipkin says about listening as well as watching—he puts a baby monitor in his yard, so he can listen inside during cold months—but he's more sanguine about junk birds.

"It's true that some birds are a nuisance—like Canada Geese that've ceased to migrate because what we do gives them what they need to stay. It means more of their young survive, and that means golf courses covered with guano. But if we measured these things in terms of human value systems, starlings and pigeons would be the heroes of the bird world. They came here as immigrants—illegal immigrants, even. They looked around and said, 'works for me,' and they've been marvelously successful."

In thinking about it, he says that it seems sometimes we ask birds to represent an ideal of ourselves. Bluebirds are loving parents, sing cheerful songs, and build neat nests. Starlings are avid colonizers, and their wild success comes from doing pretty much what the early European settlers did—ousting whoever was in their way, and taking over. But birds, our symbols of the spiritual, should stand for our ideal rather than our real lives.

Still, it's a complicated issue, and human intervention can be important, at the right time and in the right way. In Michigan, cowbirds were totally displacing the kurtland warbler, and the decision to lower the number of cowbirds through trapping and relocation allowed the warbler to continue existing. "It's a matter of good stewardship," Rich says.

And that, according to a Rabbi I know, is a biblical injunction. In Genesis, where God gives humans dominion over the earth, this Rabbi said a more accurate translation of that word is *stewardship*. God gives humans not the right to rule life on the planet, but the responsibility to steward the creatures of the earth, caring for them and seeing to their well-being.

That is what the best of conservationist thinking does. It's what birdwatchers support. And it's certainly been Pete Dubacher's task for much of his life.

 NINE

Perching

Be as a bird perched on a frail branch that she feels bending beneath her, still she sings away all the same, knowing she has wings.

—*Victor Hugo*

4 P.M., Berkshire Bird Paradise

PETE IS STACKING WOOD, so I decide to wander on my own, take some pictures, look over my notes and add to them. I go to the back part of the sanctuary, right on the edge of the woods. Deer and fox and coyotes live back there, and once Pete spotted a Canadian lynx in the area, but he keeps the birds well protected from predators. Along this section there are little surprises everywhere. Unexpected plantings, stone frogs and gargoyles peering out of them. The dynamic nature of the building projects is also in evidence, with old cages in the process of being torn down and new ones being built, each caught at a halfway point toward completion.

The ground is wet and cool and strewn with forest debris. I pick up an old log and look for salamanders, but none appear. Too late in the year, I suppose. The constant bird talk ebbs and wanes but never fully goes away. If it did, I'd probably be frightened. Birds stop talking when it's important to stay really quiet. There silence isn't good news.

For a while I stop in front of a run of eagle houses and sit on a garden bench, just being. This is a good place to do that, a comfortable place to simply sit and feel your existence, in the company of other interesting lives. The eagles sit on their perches or rest out of sight. Kara, a blind golden eagle, comes close to the front and screams. Her housemate comes out and joins her, and then they both unruffle their feathers and get quiet. Kara, Pete says, is particularly aggressive, perhaps because she's blind. In general, though, he says that female eagles are more aggressive than males. "The guys are real wimps, especially during mating season. They get more assertive at nesting time, when the chicks need them."

I follow an old path that leads toward a pond, which is currently empty of birds. It was once used for ducks and geese and swans, but they have a new pond now. A series of docks, built years ago, are slowly giving way to water and weather and time. It's near a clearing I helped create years ago, when I brought a group of my University at Albany students here to spend the day breaking down brush and hauling it away. When we were done working, the students walked around with Pete to learn more about the birds. They were, well, enchanted.

"Dr. C," one of students said, "how do you find places like this?"

"Places like what?" I inquired.

"You know. Like, magic places."

Later, one of those students would find an injured young hawk on campus and go to great lengths to make sure it got out to Pete. It was, she told me, one of the high points of her college career, a moment when she felt like she did something, like she made a difference.

That, to me, called back what Rich Guthrie said. One bird's survival may not make a difference—except, of course, to the bird itself—but a young person's discovery of her connection to the natural world is crucial, because how can a people steward their environmental resources without that kind of essential and personal connection? If they lack that, they just won't care enough to bother.

For that reason, I worry when I see Pete working so hard and yet there's so much work still to be done. Pete has volunteers and the occasional paid help, but he's never had a regular staff, and most of the workload is on his shoulders. What would happen if his energy or will just gave out? He's the last resort for a lot of birds, the only one who houses vultures and ravens on this scale, and one of the few who also has the expertise to manage eagles. Not to mention that he has a few thousand school kids stop by every year, providing opportunities for all of them to make their own connections to nature.

As I'm contemplating this, Pete swings by on his way to the emus and tells me I'm wanted inside for dinner. He looks as energetic as he did this morning, which is reassuring. "My Dad wants to feed you," he tells me.

"Are you going in?"

"In awhile," he says. "I've got a little more to do, and I have to bring Elizabeth to a school dance. Her mom's working, so I'm the chauffer. You go on in."

"Sure," I say, and I make my way to the house with a little trepidation, thinking of my earlier attempts at conversation.

When I enter the house William is at the stove and Christine setting the table. She turns to me and beams, and the truth comes out.

"Oh, so funny," she says. "We thought you were our visiting nurse. You're the *writer*." She laughs at herself. "And here I am, telling you my illnesses." Behind her, at the stove, William chuckles along.

I laugh along with them, though I'm somewhat chagrined. Was it arrogance or humility that kept me from introducing myself properly? I'll figure that out later. For now, I'm just relieved to know the nature of the mix-up. "I should have said something," I say apologetically. She shrugs, I shrug. I ask if I can help with supper.

"No, no. We are doing this. Sit, please sit."

She hustles me in to a seat and William turns to me. "Do you like pasta?" he asks.

"I was raised on it. My mom's Italian."

His eyebrows go up a notch. "We'll see if mine measures up."

While they're getting food to the table I take a good look around. The dim light, the mingled scent of sauce and garlic, the knick-knicks that look to be from another era—I feel like I'm in my grandmother's house. Religious pictures here and there make that feeling even more pointed, as I remember my grandmother's carefully kept icons, and how, every day, she would lie down on the couch after lunch, rosary in hand, and *General Hospital* on the TV.

Christine Dubacher is also a woman of faith, raised Lutheran in Germany. She was trained as a *kinderflagen*—someone who teaches children—and had aspirations to become a missionary, going to foreign countries to work with children, but her mother talked her out of it. Oddly enough, she ended up not too far from her goal, in a foreign country, with creatures that need a lot of care. And she retains her strong faith, keeping her own set of icons on a bureau in their makeshift bedroom.

The kitchen, however, is more of a tribute to William, with both an electric stove and a woodburning cookstove from the 1800s, a clock that has horses instead of numbers, and various memorabilia such as his Calvary hat from World War Two.

He is of Swiss extraction but born in San Francisco, a five-star American veteran, meaning he took part in five major battles, including Normandy and the Battle of the Bulge. He and Christine met at the end of the war, in Czechoslovakia, where he was staff sergeant and she was helping tend the wounded with a group of young women who volunteered for this task.

He kept his eye on her, and after five days, he proposed.

"Five days," Christine tells me. "Only five, and you know what he says?"

William interrupts, speaking softly, and I hear some of Pete's kindness in his tone. "I asked her, would you like to grow old with me?"

She smiles, her face young with memory. "I decided I would," she tells me.

Anti-fraternization rules kept them apart, and William left Europe without his chosen bride. They corresponded secretly for two years, through other soldiers, and then he was able to bring her to the states and marry her. This house was their summer home, an old farm on twenty-three acres of land, most of which is woods. The Dubachers kept horses and chickens and a vegetable garden. Now they live here year-round, two exotic birds who receive special care from their son and daughter-in-law. And from their story, I begin to understand that Pete comes by his persistence honestly. It's in his blood.

William serves me a plate of pasta heaped with meat sauce. I'm fussy about pasta, having been raised on the real thing, and I'm surprised at how good it tastes. William watches me as I eat, waiting for my verdict, which I give after the first forkful.

"You know how to make sauce," I say.

He gives a brief, secret smile. "They always said I put too much garlic," he says demurely.

"I don't know if there's any such thing."

"He is a chef, you know," Christine chimes in. "He was executive chef for United Airlines."

I knew that, but I didn't think he continued to cook. Apparently, he does. I plow through the pasta, followed by apple pie with a crust to die for, and Christine and William tell me more about their lives. William's job brought him and his family to live in Honolulu when Peter was little, and from Honolulu to New Jersey, and from New Jersey to Long Island, where William worked out of what was then Idlewild airport.

He was in charge of big events—executive and star-studded dinners, the gourmet flights of the late 1960s. He fed Johnny Carson and Bobby Kennedy and more. He had a personal letter from Johnny Carson, complimenting him on his food.

"I'd like to see that," I say.

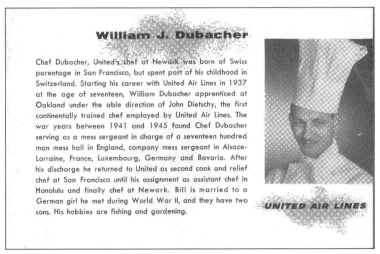

WILLIAM DUBACHER, THE DEBONAIR CHEF.

"I threw it away," he sighs.

"Wow," I shake my head. "You could've sold that on eBay for a pretty penny."

"Story of my life." I see a slow grin forming.

William kept his menus, however, which he shows me along with clippings of newspaper ads for the gourmet flights he was in charge of. A much younger William smiles out of them, leaning forward, welcoming folks to his table. He's incredibly debonair. He gets out a photo of Christine from that same era. She is beautiful, with a bright smile and smokey blue eyes. They were a dashing couple. They still are. In spite of health problems and the years passing, the brightness remains.

I'm sipping coffee and perusing a book of recipes that William still has—all very classic French cuisine—when Pete comes in to collect Elizabeth for her dance. She bounces down the stairs, dressed in bright colors, her hair done up in casual disarray that I know took some time to achieve. She looks like a magazine ad for young fun. Her mother, I think, would be proud, though Pete looks mildly astonished.

He says he'll eat when he comes back. "We can talk then," he tells me. "You getting good information from my parents?"

"Plenty of it," I say.

Elizabeth is already out the door, making her escape to the world of teenage dances, and Pete follows after.

When he's gone, I look to Christine and William again. "Do you think you did something when you raised Pete that inspired him to run a bird sanctuary?" I ask.

Christine shrugs uncertainly. "We always had a love of the nature world," she tells me. "We had the horses here, and the garden."

"Did you have birds then?"

"Of course. I love birds," William says, subduing a grin. "But mostly I love them without their feathers. They're easier to cook that way."

He has a bit of the trickster in him. Christine tut-tuts him softly, but after sixty-one years of marriage, I'm sure she's used to it. They have their own conversational rhythm, the way married couples and old friends do. At times they both talk at once, about totally different things. They don't raise their voices, and they don't seem to think either one is interrupting. They just both keep talking persistently to me, while I turn my head from one to the other, trying to listen in stereo. This is not a competition. It's just that they each have something definite to say, and are ready to say it.

As I ask repeatedly about Pete's upbringing, seeking clues to what made him take on a task as big as the Berkshire Bird Paradise, they look at me with mild bewilderment. "The birds need care, and so he cares for them," Christine tells me.

"He wanted to do this," William says. "It's his life."

Pete's choices, the way they live, the way their family lives— that's all as natural to them as a rain and sun. Just as William knew the woman of his choice within days and was willing to spend years waiting for her, Pete knows who he is and what he has to do with his life. They are a family who believes in making definite choices, and living them. They are people who problem-solve their way through ill-health and building bird houses. They like things *just* so.

William and Christine didn't have to teach Pete anything. Their own lives modeled a set of values that included doing something definite with your life, finding a task and seeing it done. And part of that definite, determined lifestyle includes valuing life in all forms, and seeing yourself as responsible for its care

"Some people think we should make this place fancy, or clean up the woods, but why?" Christine, who likes everything *just* so, comments. "This place, it does not belong to us. It belongs to the creatures who live here. The birds and the creatures of the woods. They are God's children, and now it's our job to care for them. You see?"

Yes. I most certainly do.

TEN

Bird Words

> You must not know too much, or be too precise or scientific about birds and trees and flowers and water-craft; a certain free margin, and even vagueness—perhaps ignorance, credulity—helps your enjoyment of these things.
>
> —*Walt Whitman*

Kathie Russo's husband, Spalding Gray, was best known for delivering monologues onstage—like "Monster in a Box," and "Swimming to Cambodia." On January 10, 2004, he went missing. Two months later, his body was pulled out of the East River. In this episode Kathie tells the story of the night he disappeared, and about how for three consecutive days a little bird visited her house, and seemed to be delivering a message from Spalding.

"The first image that came to my head was of Spalding obsessively circling the island, talking to himself in total anguish. . . . The second though I had was, was this a message from Spalding? We never had a bird in our house before. And I remembered the Irish had a saying that if you find a bird in your house after a person dies, if the bird is alive, their soul is free."

> —*This American Life*
> *Episode 369: Poultry Slam*
> *28 November 2008*

LONG AGO, the Iroquois say, the people lived in the sky, under the shelter of a beautiful tree. One day, a pregnant woman, wife to a chief, dreamed the tree was uprooted. It was a powerful dream, so the people did as it said and pulled up the tree.

The woman looked down through the hole left behind and there, far below, she saw a wondrous blue planet, spinning in space, shining and new. She leaned more to see it better, and then leaned further again. She leaned so far she fell, tumbling through space.

The birds who lived in the waters of the world below saw her, and two swans flew up to catch her, bringing her down safely onto the back of the turtle.

This story, a piece of the Iroquois creation story, recognizes that birds were here before us and tells us that they're friends, willing to help us journey from one realm to another, bringing us safely to ground. It's one of many places where birds appear in folktale, myth, and history as helpers to humans. Such stories remind us that our psyches are deeply rooted in the cycles of nature, its rhythms and creatures. Connection with birds is one manifestation of those roots.

Among the Greeks, Athena was associated with owls. In Hebrew folklore, Lilith, a woman who was created before Eve but who had an independent streak and left the Garden, was associated with night hawks. In Aztec mythology, Huitzilo-pochtli, god of war, death, and the sun, is often described as a hummingbird. His father was a ball of feathers, and his mother was Coatlicue, the goddess who also gave birth to the moon and stars.

Often, in folktales and myths, birds serve the same purpose they do in spiritual realms. They are messengers, harbingers, guides between worlds and go-betweens for the gods. Other times, they offer a clear lesson: if you're good to birds, they'll return the favor.

In a Scottish tale of three daughters who are going out to seek their fortune, two of the daughters refuse to share their bread with a mother quail and her twelve quail pups. The mother quail curses them, and they are ultimately killed and thrown on a garbage heap. The third daughter shares her bread with the birds, and as she sleeps in the woods that night the mother quail and her pups gather around her, fluffing their feathers and cooing softly. She not only sleeps warm and well, she goes on to find her fortune and bring her less charitable sisters back from the dead.

You might say that Pete Dubacher is a living illustration of these folktales, setting a good example to us all, because in larger terms it's absolutely true that when we take care of the planet and its creatures, the planet continues to give us what we need to live. When we're out of balance with that, of course, the bad results rebound against us.

The late poet and activist Tom Nattell expressed this in one of his own poems, which I saw him read at an event he organized called "Readings Against the End of the World." This benefit for nuclear disarmament groups was a marathon event, the readings and performances going on for twenty-four hours straight. At one of them, Tom got on stage at about 2 A.M., and started whirling hollow pink plastic tubes around his head. They whined and whistled as he bellowed out, "Save the whales! Save the Trees! Save the Eagles!"

After a lengthy litany, he ended by shouting out, "Save my ass!"

Yes. When we save something else, we're also saving ourselves. So the old stories and the new poets say.

Birds in folktales are also often embodiments of wandering souls, the spellbound and the dead. In an Eastern European tale called "The Juniper Tree," a woman stands in front of a juniper tree and wishes for a son. She quickly becomes pregnant, but then dies giving birth and is buried beneath the tree she loved.

Her husband, overcome with grief, marries someone else. His second wife isn't a very nice woman, and she doesn't like her stepson. She kills him, and sets up his death so that her own daughter, Marjorie, thinks she's done the dirty deed. Grief-stricken and horrified, Marjorie gathers up her brother's bones and buries them under the juniper tree, which immediately begins to shudder and shake until, at its very top, a beautiful bird appears, and flies away. Though she's not sure why, Marjorie feels deeply consoled.

The bird goes flying about the town, stopping to sing for different people. In payment, he's given a pair of shoes from the cobbler, a necklace from the smith, and a millstone from the miller. He returns to Marjorie's house and gives her the shoes, gives the father the necklace, and then drops the millstone on the stepmother's head, killing her.

After this, he is transformed back into the little boy he once was, and the family is reunited, minus the stepmother.

I'll admit, it's an odd story, but I like the connection between mother and tree and boy and bird. It's a living web of interaction that creates justice. And, like many stories, the bird serves the purpose of containing the soul until it can find its human body once more.

To me, that makes a great deal of sense. If you believe in a human spirit, it must have all the ephemeral fragility and the thirty-million-year endurance of birds. Even if you don't believe in a human spirit, certainly birds are also an appropriate metaphor for the flitting wings of our imagination, our capacity to see beyond our own lives to something else. That may be why so many of our imaginings are expressed in terms of our relationship with birds. And that may be how birds help connect us to a larger environmental awareness.

Karen Purcell, who works on the Cornell Urban Bird Project, believes this is so. The goal of the project is to encourage people to really see what's outside their window, whether they live in the city or the country or the suburbs. To do so, they provide small grants and other support for nature celebrations of all different kinds, from making nature inspired quilts to art exhibits to dance and poetry events. Some of these celebrations are as simple as bringing people to the Harlem Mere in the northern part of Central Park and asking them to look around.

"We did that once, and the first thing I saw was a black-crowned night heron, right there in New York City. It was wonderful," Karen says.

The mini-grants they award for celebrations allow each community to create its celebration in its own way, according to the community's needs and environment. They also encourage people, through their website, to connect art and birds.

"If you go out and are inspired by something—a pigeon or a hawk or whatever brings emotion to you, you can send us a picture or a video or a piece of embroidery. That combines people's observations with their expressions, and that's good. We can't love the environment unless we're attached to it imaginatively and expressively. Once that happens, people really begin to look, and that's the beginning of love."

Nature writer and high school teacher Bill Danielson would agree. His columns, which include "Speaking of Nature" written for the Albany Times Union, are all about the small and interesting details that wildlife offers to our imagination, and he came to love those details in part through his own imagination.

His mom always had a birdfeeder, but when he was young he had more interest in World War Two fighter planes than birds. Then a second-grade teacher suggested to him that instead of drawing warplanes, he should draw birds. He grew up in a house where Christmas and birthday presents were homemade, and there were only so many warplane drawings he could give away, so he started painting and carving birds instead. "They were easier to draw than animals," he told me. "Fur is a pain in the butt."

Through drawing birds, he began to see them in a new way. Now he believes that it's important to nurture a connection of the heart as well as the mind, developing interactions that are imaginative and emotional through art and play as well as science.

"I was influenced a lot by books and movies. The whole Disney thing, with the little animals who help you. And my mom took us to Laughing Brook, home of Thorton Burgess, who wrote a zillion books about the animals that lived there—Paddy the Beaver, Sammy Jay, and Old Man Coyote. Once every few weeks I was allowed to pick out one of them. It was a big deal to me."

That helped him connect with animals and birds on an emotional level. He doesn't romanticize it the way he did when he was young, but he still thinks of his relationship with birds as personal, and daily. "How can you not feel that way?" he says. "If someone brings you a nest of baby blue jays—just the sweetest, funniest little creatures. They bicker and cause trouble and are so much fun. How could you not be personally attached?"

His deck is peppered with birdfeeders, his land peppered with birdhouses. In his kitchen is a clock that has birds instead of numbers. He puts out seed as soon as he wakes up, before he has his own breakfast.

"I figure they're hungrier than I am, so they eat first," he says.

A licensed rehabber, one of his favorite birds was his crow, Mr. Crow, found as a baby. He was driving up to a tollbooth off the turnpike when he spotted a little crow standing in the center of the road. He managed to straddle it with his wheels, then pulled over and went back, got it and brought it home.

When the crow was old enough, he released it, but it was injured in the wild and returned to him with a condition called bumblefoot. To keep him off his feet while the injury rested and healed, Mr. Crow stayed in a sling made from an embroidery hoop. Bored with confinement, he became a bit of a thief. An unattended wallet was to be opened all contents removed. He also stole spoons so he could drop them off the side of the porch, apparently just for the aesthetic experience.

"He'd watch them, and you could almost hear him saying, 'Oh, now, that was a good one,'" Bill says.

Stories of animals and birds were one of the sparks that helped create the relationship he has now with such creatures. And, he says, that's still of interest to young people. "The number one requested movie in my high school is *Finding Nemo*. The kids love it. It's colorful, funny, has a lot of fish. What more could you ask for?"

Nurturing that kind of connection is, he thinks, very different from indoctrination to environmental correctness. "You can pay lip service forever to doing the right thing environmentally, but unless you're in touch with your environment, why would you really care?"

I remember this from my own childhood. Along with my hours spent roaming the local woods, Mutual of Omaha and Walt Disney both fostered my interest in what was wild. I still remember the Disney movie *The Three Lives of Thomasina*, which tells the story of a Scottish girl whose cat dies at the hands of her widowed veterinarian father. Their difficult relationship is repaired with the return of Thomasina and the help of a beautiful and mysterious woman who is a bit of a witch, with powers to revive and heal animals.

I envied that woman's relationship with animals, and longed for the ability to understand them as she did. As a result, I sought contact with birds and animals, hoping to blend human and non-human experience, hoping to meet, with understanding, a consciousness other than my own. That, I think, is a fundamental yearning of humans, for many reasons. So does Bill.

He still finds the clarity of nature a wonderful relief in a world filled with hype. "It's pleasurable and calming. It's honest. Except for blue jays and squirrels, there's not a lot of greed or hidden agendas. They're here because they're hungry or thirsty. That's all. They don't worry about taxes or bills. So much of our arbitrarily imposed rigor screws up our day. Being with birds reminds you that it's arbitrary after all."

We are storytelling creatures, learning through telling and listening to stories more easily, perhaps, than any other way because stories are capable of containing both fact and heart. Because of that, stories can be the best way for young people to understand and connect with nature. The old stories were often told to do just that. The new stories still do the same.

Recently my eight-year-old nephew, Nicolas, came to visit. It was deep summer and the fireflies were in full swing, and we took a walk alone in the fields behind my house, which were saturated with tiny dancing lights. It was one of those magical moments that inspires confidences, and Nicolas said to me, "I think I love everything that's wild."

"Do you?" I asked, and he nodded somberly. He told me about a book he'd been reading, one of a series by A. K. Applegate, called *Animorphs*. In the series, some people can morph into different animals. He was especially fond of the boy who could become a hawk.

"I think sometimes I am a hawk," he said very seriously. "I feel it. I feel wings, and I see things the way they do."

"That's good," I say, hoping I'm encouraging relationship rather than fantasy.

He nodded, still very serious, then looked up at me. "Did you ever wonder what a mouse tastes like?"

I had to admit, I hadn't.

The night grew deeper and we went inside to the more mundane world of popcorn and Disney DVDs, but I was glad that Nicolas had already developed enough of a relationship with the wild world to ask a question like that. Along with Bill, I believe that responsible and positive interaction with nonhumans grows out of a love fostered at that level. Something that goes beyond asking what the planet can do for us, and moves into thinking about what the world is, in and of itself.

The Berkshire Bird Paradise is a good place to do that, both by day and by night.

ELEVEN

Raising the Young

'Pan, who and what art thou?' [Hook] cried huskily.
'I'm youth, I'm joy,' Peter answered at a venture, 'I'm a
little bird that has broken out of the egg.'
—*James M. Barrie*

10 P.M., Berkshire Bird Paradise

ALL IS QUIET. Dark and quiet. Pete's out stoking woodstoves, and I'm in my room for the night. It has the sloping ceilings of a finished attic space, has an old world feel to it. The bedding is pink, and foofy. All of it is *just* so, carefully arranged and tended.

Before Elizabeth went off to her dance she brought me up here to show me where to put my bags, and I spent some time talking with her. She's a typical teenager, involved in her social life more than anything else right now.

"What was it like growing up here?" I asked.

She shrugged. "It was fun. I liked all the birds."

"Your friends didn't think it was weird?"

"No. They thought it was kind of cool."

"And now? Is it different?"

"Well, yeah. Now I can say the name right. When I was a kid, I couldn't."

I'm sure she thinks I'm asking questions that are, like, kind of weird, y'know? She can't really understand what I mean when I ask if it was unusual, or if it changed her, living here. It's all she's ever known. And she's a teenager, more interested in her future than her past.

95

When I ask what she wants that to look like, she's more definite. "I want to live in the suburbs," she tells me, definite and
clear. "Somewhere that has birds, and trees, and all that, but it's
closer to shopping. I think I might go into real estate. I like
houses."

I think of Georgi, who told me that she was always rescuing
birds when she was a child, but that all went away in her teenage
years, not returning again until she was a young adult. I had the
same experience. As a teenager, the only wildlife I was interested
in were boys. But the birds returned to me, and to Georgi. My
guess is that Elizabeth will always have birds in her life as well.
Her mother tells me she was imprinted for it even before she was
born.

Betty Ann also tells me that her arrival was quite a surprise.
She and Pete were married on October 10th, and on November
14th she took a pregnancy test that came out positive. She went
to Pete and told him.

"That's good," he said, manlike.

"No," she told him. "You don't understand. I'm *pregnant*."

Once she got over the initial shock, however, Betty Ann says
the experience was deeply spiritual. Deeply good.

To others, it might also seem deeply different. During her
pregnancy, they had quite a few emu eggs hatch, and Betty Ann
took in the ones that weren't doing very well. Two of them regularly slept on her burgeoning belly, one on either side, during
that time. She didn't think they'd survive, but she wanted at least
to give them what comfort and warmth she could while they
were around.

They did survive, however, and these same two emus, when
grown, would flank young Elizabeth as she toddled about the
place, always on either side of her as friendly, protective sen-
tinels. Betty Ann says Elizabeth didn't really know what species
she was for quite a few years.

"It took me forever to potty train her. Then, at meals, she'd
squat under the table to eat. She'd stick her head in the tank with
the emus to drink. But when other kids came around she was the
one to reassure them if they were afraid. Elizabeth knew her
birds at an early age, knew instinctively which ones to approach,
which ones to leave alone."

PETE'S FLEDGLING EAGLES.

She's growing up now, and Betty Ann takes that process philo-sophically. "Everything needs a mother, and then, when it's time to go, they go. I had a crow, Bubba, who followed me around. He was great. But eventually, he flew away. That's what they do, and that's really what you want for them. That they'll find their own lives."

But birds return, often going back to nest where they were born. I wonder what Elizabeth's return will look like. I have no doubt that her parents will fledge her well, and release her into the wild when it's time. After all, they've managed to do that with all kinds of nestlings, including eagles, something that hardly anyone else has managed to do.

 TWELVE

$\mathcal{L}ike\ \mathcal{E}agle$

- Causes of death in eagles—Fatal gun shot wounds, electrocution, poisoning, collisions with vehicles, and starvation.
- Bald eagles have 7,000 feathers.
- Bald eagles can fly to an altitude of 10,000 feet. During level flight, they can achieve speeds of about 30 to 35 mph.

—www.baldeagleinfo.com

. . . . Like Eagle, that Sunday morning over Salt River,
Circled in blue sky, in wind,
Swept our hearts clean with sacred wings.
We see you, see ourselves,
And know that we must take the utmost care and kindness
In all things.
Breathe in, knowing we are made of all this,

—From Eagle Poem, Joy Harjo

IN THE MID-1990S, two hunters were hiking the wilds of Alaska when they spotted a bear by a nearby stream. This bear wasn't prey, however. It was predator, attacking a bald eagle that was searching the same stream for salmon. The hunters switched into rescue mode, scared the bear away, and retrieved the eagle, which had a badly injured wing. They tucked it into one of the backpacks and zipped it up, leaving only the head visible. Then they brought it to a Juneau raptor center for care.

The eagle, now known as Zipper because of his backpack ride, had his wing tended. It seemed like he'd never fly again, however, so he was sent to his permanent home, at the Berkshire Bird Paradise.

When Pete got him he was still healing, and there was an awful moment when the powerful muscles of the bird ripped out his stitches. The bird was in danger of bleeding to death and Pete had no time to get a vet, so he did the restitch himself, using everything he'd learned about bird anatomy to make sure he was working with the musculature rather than against it. This time the repair held. Zipper survived and still makes his home at the sanctuary, along with seven other bald eagles, and two golden eagles. And Pete's reputation as an eagle man grew.

His eagles are all permanent residents, too injured to ever leave. Battle-scarred veterans of the Industrial Revolution, they acquired their wounds in a number of different ways. The bald eagle known as General Schwartzkopf, (aka, The General) was soaring over the airport in Moab, Utah, when an airplane hit him. Thor flew into a power line. Olympia was hit by a car in Alaska. Eddie was shot during his fledgling flight. Yet another eagle was injured in the Exxon Valdez oil spill.

Pete's two golden eagles come from Buttonwood Zoo in Massachusetts, which had to get rid of animals when they were rebuilding. The birds would have been euthanized if Pete didn't take them in. That often happens and Pete has become a court of last resort for such zoo birds.

"That's one of the problems with zoos," Pete says. "They have to think in terms of economics. If an animal isn't a big draw they often have to get another animal instead. They need their animals to generate revenue. That means they have to euthanize. I don't."

By 1992, he had ten eagles, all of which would have been dead without the Berkshire Bird Paradise. Their arrival is usually an exciting event, since they come in injured, and often from far away. Once, Pete got a phone call from Anchorage, Alaska, from a place that had several eagles who needed sanctuary. The problem was how to get them to Pete. Did he have any ideas?

He did. He called J. T. Weeker, then head of the U.S. Postal service. "The Big Kahuna," as Pete describes him. Weeker called a smaller kahuna in Anchorage, who saw to it that four eagles arrived at the Berkshire Bird Sanctuary within twenty-four hours. One of them, Olympia, became the official mascot of the U.S. Postal service.

By the mid-1990s, Pete had enough eagles to begin thinking about the possibility of raising chicks. Most bird experts thought that was wishful thinking on his part, because eagles are notoriously difficult to breed in captivity. They'll lay eggs, but either the eggs won't hatch, or the parents won't care for them and the nestlings quickly die. But eagles were once prolific residents of this country, and it seemed important to Pete to do his part to support their return.

The bald eagle was officially adopted as the U.S. national emblem on June 20, 1782, and now it appears on the National Seal, bearing an olive branch in one talon and thirteen arrows in the other. This image, however, grows from an earlier source— the Iroquois confederacy. In their history, they tell how the Peacemaker drew their people together as a unified group. He made them try to break a bundle of arrows, as a metaphor to explain how their strength was much greater as a group than as single nations. The Peacemaker planted a Tree of Peace, and said the Eagle would perch on its top, to guard their newly found peace.

It's estimated that before European settlers arrived, eagles here numbered half a million. They declined as human population increased, destroying their habitat and competing for the same fish and game that they consumed. They were also hunted, particularly by Alaskan fisherman, who killed around one hundred thousand between 1917 and 1953, because they believed eagles interfered with their salmon fishing. Then, DDT came along as a popular pesticide, decreasing their fertility, harming the adults, and thinning their eggshells enough that not many survived. By the 1960s, we were down to an estimated 417 nesting pairs of bald eagles. In 1967 they were officially declared an endangered species in states south of the fortieth parallel, but it wasn't until 1976 that they were placed on the U.S. Fish and Wildlife Service's list of endangered species.

The question then became, how to bring them back. Besides the improbable breeding and release, there were two possibilities—egg stealing and hacking.

Eagles sometimes lay more than two eggs, but generally only two per nest survive. Conservationists have learned that they can take the extra eaglet egg from the nest and place them with an adult pair whose eggs are infertile. Sometimes, the eagles will raise such a chick as their own. Alternatively, conservationists can "hack" a nest, waiting until all the eggs hatch, then taking the extra eaglet away and putting it in a human made nest, where it's fed by humans who stay out of sight. At around twelve weeks, when the fledglings are ready to leave the nest, the enclosure around it is opened and the birds are free to fly. Food is provided until it's clear that the birds have learned to fend for themselves.

Habitat loss remains an issue, and though the numbers are certainly not what they were before Europeans arrived on the continent, these reintroduction efforts have proven remarkably successful, bringing the number of nesting pairs up to eighty for New York State and more than four thousand for the United States, most of which live in Alaska.

Six of those New York State eagles—four bald and two golden—are from the Berkshire Bird Paradise, bred and raised by eagles who are blind or have only one wing. Nobody thought Pete could do it, least of all himself.

It took a long time, and some patience, he tells me. At first, he didn't even know how to identify the different sexes, so he put them in an aviary and watched them carefully. "One thing—the female's always bigger," Pete told me. "Don't ask me why. There's plenty of theories but nobody really knows. Then, I saw how they behaved with each other, and I knew who was paired up. Eagles mate for life, so I guess they take their time, too."

In this way, he watched as they chose their mates, then gave them their own private dwelling places, built to please any self-respecting eagle. The building, he said, was important. "You have to study what you're building for, find out how they live, what they need. One of the biggest mistakes people make is to try and build something people oriented rather than bird- or animal-oriented."

Since his birds are disabled, he has to take into account their particular injuries as well, and make sure they're safe from predators. Like any creature, they want a sense of safety, and some privacy. "One thing that I've learned," Pete says, "if you feed them well, build them a proper environment, and give them a good space, there's very little you have to do because, keep in mind, they know how to take care of themselves. And they don't want to be hovered over and constantly bothered," he adds. "That can be very stressful. Sometimes the best way to calm them down is to give them their space."

His aeries, resembling megalithic tree houses, certainly do that.

Even so, for quite a few years nothing much happened. The birds would lay eggs, and they wouldn't hatch. Hopes rose and fell. Then, one cold morning, he climbed up into the nest in one of the aeries and saw two little heads sticking out. He could barely believe it.

He called Peter Nye, an eagle specialist with the Department of Conservation, who developed the hacking procedure. He also didn't believe it. Nye came out to the sanctuary, and Pete just watched as he walked up the ladder to the nest. Up at the top, Nye grinned, and Pete knew exactly how he felt.

The baby eagles flourished and eventually had what's called a light release right at the sanctuary. That's simply opening the door of their enclosure and letting them do what they choose.

"They're really fun to watch at that point," Pete says. "They do a short flight out to a tree, and then come back. They go exploring a little further, and come back again. They're like little teenagers, seeing what they can do, but they still want that nest in sight. Then, eventually, they just go."

His birds are banded and tracked, and in 2008 he got a picture from Peter Nye of one of them feeding at a pond in Sullivan County. That, he says, was a special moment, as were the two eagle chicks he released in Vermont around Lake Champlain as part of a federal program.

"Even though my life can seem kind of dull—cleaning up pigeon water and tossing dead rats to birds seven days a week—I put those eagles out there," Pete says. "That's a great thing to know. It feels just great."

Pete has also released golden eagles, which tend to get less airtime than our national bird. But these magnificent birds, with their seven-foot wing span and three-foot-long bodies, were residents of New York State as recently as a hundred years ago. Human encroachment pushed them out, diminishing their hunting area, but Pete has returned two more to of these great birds to the wild, bred from two of his permanently injured eagles. Dottie and Daphne—the latter named after Fred LeBrun's niece, who had recently been killed in a car accident. She flew off in 2004, and Pete continued to see her flying around the sanctuary for some time after her release.

The parents of these chicks, along with the bald eagle parents, remain as residents of the sanctuary, and may raise more young for release. They could live another twenty years, and as they age, just like humans they'll need more care. Eagles often develop a physical problem similar to hip dysplasia in dogs. Then they have to live inside and be kept warm through the winter.

That's what happened to the eagle Martell, who arrived in 1990. As he grew older he could no longer walk, though he could still stand. So Pete gave him an indoor residence, with Astroturf that got hosed down as needed. He lived inside for a few years, then one day when Pete was walking by he just fell over. Pete picked him up and cradled him in his arms.

"I was holding him and slowly petting his head, and he just went to sleep and that was it," Pete says. "They trust me, and how do you walk away from that?"

When I hear stories like that, Pete seems to good to be true. We live in a cynical age, a world that sees corporate interests as much more powerful than the good of the people, much less the birds, and a world where many institutions—private and government—exist to serve themselves rather than their public.

And here is a man who values the life of a bird enough to provide nursing-home care for it. At the same time, the bird trusts him enough to let him cradle him as he dies. Could it possibly be real, just as it seems? For answers, I went to a man known for his impatience with any illusion or trickery, and for a particularly sharp tongue.

I went to the chief pathologist of New York State's Department of Environmental Conservation, Dr. Ward Stone.

 THIRTEEN

Ward Stone

THE PLAIN, rather industrial-looking building for the New York State Department of Environmental Conservation's Wildlife Pathology Unit sits within the Five Rivers Environmental Education Center, a good place to go birdwatching. I'd been to both Five Rivers and this office before. The office visit was to bring in a dead bat my cat, Chaos, brought in. He'd leapt up, caught the thing midair, pierced it once in the heart and ran inside to drop it in the hall, probably for our supper. I knew bats weren't easy to catch, so I was worried that it might be rabid, but testing revealed that it was just too slow.

As I entered the building I stopped in the hallway to peer at the large glass display case with its collection of bones, skins, stuffed animals and birds, an interesting greeting for visitors. But after all, it's a pathology lab. They have lots of dead things around the place.

Ward Stone's office, down the hall, is also grey and industrial-looking, the only decoration in the room a large framed display of wings on the wall behind his desk. Ward himself sits in front of a computer, and he's not what I expected to see from his voice on the phone, or his reputation. I expected someone older, taller, with very bushy eyebrows and an intimidating stance. Instead, I see a man who's average in height and build, with white hair thinning on top and a face that's too round to look mean. He wears khaki and flannel, but something about his demeanor makes it seem like he'd make an easy transition to being either a fifth-century monk or an old Mohawk chief, in Kanastoweh and regalia. I can't decide which suits him better, and that troubles me.

Yet, he has a reputation as a difficult man, honest to a fault, opinionated, not easy to please. His public profile in New York State is high, and long-lived. He's been with the DEC for forty years, and in that time has faced more than one attempt to oust him from his position when his outspokenness went against the political grain. He runs a regular show on WAMC public radio, *In Our Backyard,* and has worked with all the important issues of wildlife illness, from the poisoning of turtles by PCBs at the Akwasasne Mohawk Reservation, to West Nile disease, and much more. His interests are as varied as the environment itself. In 2008 he spoke at a Pine Bush dinner on current environmental successes and dangers, and was interviewed by the show *Capital Outsider* on the dangers of our obsessions with perfect lawns and the pesticides we use to keep them that way.

Because of that I've been a little nervous about this interview, wondering if I'd see the sharp side of his tongue, and if so, how I'd react. When I enter his office I put myself in a receptive kind of mode, ready to go with the flow.

He looks up from his computer. "How many emails do you get a day?" he asks.

"Too many," I say. "Spam rules."

"I get hundreds. Every day. And most of them aren't spam. They're important. But I don't have anyone to answer them except me."

His staff has been slashed by recent cuts. He is currently, like Pete Dubacher, a one-man show. "They're trying to push me out. Again," he says. He looks me up and down. "Are you coming from work?"

"Teaching," I tell him.

"What do you teach?"

"Right now, public speaking, writing, interpersonal communication."

He shows me a grin. "Interpersonal communication. I figured out a long time ago I didn't have a lot of skills in that, so I decided I'd better go for power instead. Lots of support from mass media and so on."

I grin back at him. I still can't settle between monk and Mohawk chief. Certainly he doesn't seem like your stereotypical state worker. Yet, he started when Five Rivers was just opening. He met Pete here, not long after, when Pete was just getting serious about the Berkshire Bird Paradise, moving it into the realm of an ongoing, certified sanctuary.

"He came to me for some advice about his birds, told me what he planned," Ward says. "I asked him about his education, and he said just high school. No degrees. And he had no money, no experience, really. I thought he didn't have a snowball's chance in hell."

Ward shakes his head at the memory. "See, he's an idealist, and they usually give up when the money and fame don't show up fast enough. But Pete was the exception to that rule. He worked at it every day, learned everything he could. He got his Ph.D. in experience. He did it without money or school."

As he tells me this, a woman with red hair enters. She's a very fast talker, and she's just delivered a vat of bat bodies for fungus testing to someplace called the Anthrax Lab. Bats, little mice with wings, a delirious combination of bird and mammal, have begun dying all over New York State, for reasons no one can yet determine. It seems to be some kind of fungus, but nobody knows what causes it, or why it's suddenly killing so many bats.

Ward asks if they're in separate bags, and the woman seems nonplussed. Ward doesn't say anything, but an eyebrow goes up, and with minimal body language he manages to convey a kind of underground rumbling anger which might explode. I suddenly see where his reputation comes from. Monk or Mohawk, he's got some personal power if not interpersonal skill.

He looks at me, shrugs, turns on his heel and heads toward the Anthrax Lab. "Should I follow or wait?" I ask.

"Wait," he says. "I'll be back."

Part of me is aching to see the Anthrax Lab and a vat of bats. I have my gruesome side. Another part is glad to let it go. Instead, I study the framed display on the wall.

The wings inside it are huge and tiny, colorful and drab, fluffy and sleek. They have in common that they're all complex. Even the raven's wing has an intricate layering you can't see when it soars by overhead. The circular russet caplet of feathers on the ring-necked-pheasant wing looks like an epaulet on a general's shoulder. Perhaps that's where it came from. We wear wings on our flightless bodies, out of envy or admiration or both.

I have time for a good long study of the wings before Ward returns, looking gruff and grim. "Everything okay?" I ask him.

"The usual," he says tersely. His phone rings before he can say more, and after he answers the question—from a woman who's been tracking a local fox with sarcoptic mange—he goes through his seventeen unheard messages for the week. "I have to," he says. "It's full. Nobody can leave a message if I don't empty it."

He's interrupted again by a call from someone who has a bat on the side of their office building. "Can you reach it with a long stick? Okay. Well, I'm interested in why he's out there because no bat should be out in this weather. Yeah. I'll try and get someone over there."

When he hangs up, he sighs. "There's too much to do. Never enough people to do it."

"Is that the general atmosphere these days? Cutbacks, and so on."

"Oh, yeah. Sometimes it seems like nobody cares anymore. Y'know, when Pete and I started up it was the seventies. We were all trying to save the earth. I was going after DDT, and Pete was taking care of birds. We expected society to be different about the environment by now. Where are all the people who care? It's all politics."

He waves it away. He's been dealing with it for forty years, riding out one political maelstrom after another. His advice to Pete has always been to avoid it however he can, and Pete has taken that to heart. For instance, he was asked to bring an eagle to the Democratic National Convention for Bill Clinton, but then counted the cost. Going would put him in a political camp, and whether it was one he liked or not, someday that might come back and bite him. "Keep it simple and stupid," Pete told me. "That's what you have to do sometimes. I stay out of politics."

Ward, in his position, can't dance that way.

"Some people still care," I point out. "You, for instance. And Pete."

"Pete," he says, "is unique. His kind of extreme dedication usually only exists to support the American philosophy of greed. People work hard to get rich. But Pete cares about life. He has the drive and interest to keep it going, too. "

"Is that why he's been so successful with breeding the eagles?" I ask.

"That's pretty much it. He cares about them. Every day he sees that they eat what they need, even if he doesn't. Every day. He treats his friends the same way. It's really daily care, paying attention. That long-term commitment."

For some reason, the Mohawk keep making appearances in my mind. Now I think of the Iroquois philosophy that says actions should be weighed with a concern for how they'll affect the next seven generations from your own. Pete sees the world that way. Ward does, too.

"You've been here a long time. You made that kind of commitment, too."

He sniffs, looks away. "Sometimes I think it's been wasted."

"What would you have done instead?"

"Science," he says, and now he looks a little wistful. "Pure research. In a lab at Harvard or Yale."

That would be his monkish side. The thinker, cloistered with knowledge. "You would have been missed here," I point out.

For this, I get a little grin. I'm not flattering, though. I like what he has to say on the radio, and I've looked into some of his research. Curmudgeon and thorn in the state's side he may be, but he cares, and he's spent time researching things that others probably wouldn't touch. I read about his research at the Akwasasne Mohawk reservation, where people, plants, and animals were poisoned by toxic waste from Alcoa, Reynolds, and General Motors. "That was important work," I say.

"You know about that?" he asks, surprised.

"I read about it when I was doing research for a different project, on the Peacemaker story."

"I'm part Mohawk," he tells me. "My ancestors on one side go back to the earliest European settlers. The other side's Mohawk."

Well, I think. My instincts are better than I knew.

He takes out his wallet, opens it. "Here, look," he says, and shows me pictures of his children. One of them could have stepped out of a portrait of a young British child. The other looks pure Mohawk. "Wow," I say. "The genetic roll of the dice."

"Yeah. Isn't that something? You know Tom Porter? Jake Swamp?"

I've met Tom at Kanatsiohareke, the traditional Mohawk community he founded in Fonda, New York. And I've met Jake, former Mohawk sub-chief and founder of the Tree of Peace Society. They're both men like Ward and Pete, who do important work in the world in quiet, persistent ways. "I know them," I tell Ward.

"Great people, right? Also struggling with what they're trying to do. Seems like all the best people are always struggling."

"You think Pete struggles?"

He considers. "He certainly works. Damn hard, everyday. That's where his success with the eagles comes from. Y'know, he named one of the chicks after my daughter—a daughter I had who died. Teresa Rose. That eagle chick—that's her spirit, soaring free. Look. I'll show you something."

He goes to a corner of the office that's cluttered with files and books, and pulls up a colorfully painted wood carving, about four inches square. It has a sun at the center, animals, birds, and plants surrounding it.

"I made that for her. One night, I just started doing it, and I couldn't stop until it was done. These are all the spirits she's with now. Everything that's part of her."

It's beautiful, and unexpected. Somewhere between the monk and the Mohawk there's an artist here as well. I suppose I shouldn't be surprised. Pete paints watercolors and carves totem poles. Both men, burly, strong guys who work like hell for what they believe in, also carve delicate works of art for their daughters.

I'm more moved than I dare say by what I see. I think I understand Pete better by knowing the people he draws to him. Like his parents, they are definite, with definite ideas and goals. They believe in work and problem solving. They commit. They make art for their daughters. All of that requires a profound hope, the kind of hope that can get badly battered, but can't ever be utterly relinquished. Not while breath remains. It's inherent in their beings, the same way grass is green. It may not be the easiest way to live, but it's probably the best.

"The thing about Pete," Ward says, "is that his dedication to birds and to life in general is a model of caring about nature and animals. What he does sets an example for the world. That may be his biggest contribution, and he doesn't even know it."

Et tu, Ward, I think. Et tu.

 FOURTEEN

Holding Up the Earth

There was a strange stillness. The birds, for example—
where had they gone? . . . It was a spring without voices.
On the mornings that had once throbbed with the dawn
chorus of robins, catbirds, doves, jays, wrens, and scores
of other bird voices there was now no sound; only
silence lay over the fields and woods and marsh.
—"Introduction," *Silent Spring*, Rachel Carson

ONE COLD AND SNOWY DAY in late February, when I despaired of spring, my husband called me to the window.

"What kind of birds are those?" he asked, pointing to a huddled group on a branch of our Shagbark hickory tree. "They look like sparrows, but they're kind of a funny color."

I looked. There were maybe ten small birds, with dark backs and russet colored fronts. The snow was coming down hard, and they sat puffed into feathery balls, looking peeved. As the wind shifted and light fell on their backs, I got a better look, and then I gasped.

"They're bluebirds!" I exclaimed.

"No," my husband said. "No way."

"Yes, way," I insisted.

We got the binoculars, and sure enough, they were a huddled mass of bluebirds, riding out the storm in the branches of our tree. I'd never seen even one, much less a whole flock. I wondered if my husband and I were having a joint hallucination brought on by too much winter.

But they were real. And they stayed in our tree for many weeks, feeding on the suet we put out. Some time in April they began clustering in pairs, and then they disappeared into the woods. I thought I knew what they were doing there, and I was glad, because it meant there would be even more bluebirds next year.

Their arrival, in the middle of a blizzard, helped me ride out the remainder of that winter. Even though I still had to shovel, and the heating bill didn't go down any, and I didn't win the lottery, we felt blessed by their presence in an essential way. Maybe because they're such elusive birds, even though they're the state bird of New York. They were named that in 1970, when DDT, habitat destruction, and the increase of starlings and house sparrows who compete with them had lowered their numbers so much that one delegate objected, saying, "I think this is a bit premature. After all, who has ever seen a bluebird, except perhaps on the cover of a greeting card?"

They're making a comeback, though, partly because of a strong campaign for bluebird houses to replace lost nesting habitat. By the time they were elected the state bird, the Bluebird Recovery Program had supplied more than twelve thousand people with copies of plans for the nestbox invented by Dick Peterson, and David Ahlgren had shipped out over sixty thousand ready made or in kits (*Bluebird* 22:.3, Summer 2000). If that campaign hadn't happened, I might now be telling you about a time when beautiful bluebirds sang in our trees, instead of taking pictures of them in my backyard.

The comeback of these and other bird species such as hummingbirds, eagles, and hawks after the debacle of DDT wouldn't have happened either if conservationists and concerned citizens hadn't acted in time. Unfortunately, those success stories are balanced by others that represent our egregious human failures. Consider, for instance the moa.

Moa were flightless and wingless birds who lived in New Zealand, a place that pretty much belonged to the birds for most of its existence. Here, there were no reptilian or mammalian predators. In fact, there were no mammals at all until humans arrived about a thousand years ago. Bird life developed in various and beautiful ways, and included the ten or so species known as moa, which ranged from turkey-sized birds to something resembling Big Bird. The largest weighed in at about 510 pounds.

Moas were the dominant herbivores, hunted only by Haast's eagle—another huge bird—until the Maori arrived. These new predators were apparently hungrier than the eagle, because they hunted the moa to extinction in less than a hundred years. The Haast's eagle followed soon after.

That may sound excessive, but one of the most astonishing stories of mass wildlife slaughter took place here in the United States, when early European settlers destroyed the entire population of passenger pigeons, which numbered in the billions when they arrived. Flocks of these long-tailed blue birds, swift and graceful, would take three or four hours to pass by, shadowing the sun as they went. One report from April of 1873 in Michigan notes a continuous stream flying overhead between 7:30 in the morning and 4:00 in the afternoon. Estimates are that there were about five billion of them, the total number of all birds that live here today.

Their numbers declined early on after European settlement simply because more humans were hunting them, but the real slaughter began with the practice of commercial hunting to supply east coast cities with meat. In his book *A Green History of the World*, Clive Ponting notes that three hundred thousand pigeons a year were sent just to New York in 1855. By 1860, the numbers approached madness, almost a quarter of a million were sent east from Michigan in *one day*. By 1874, Michigan was sending four hundred thousand birds a week east. Since females lay only one egg a year, numbers fell rapidly. The last known passenger pigeons were seen in the 1890s, and the last survivor of the species died in captivity in 1914 (pp. 168–170).

They are, to my mind, the *Titanic* of the bird world, a testament to human shortsightedness and greed.

Passenger pigeons aren't the only birds we wiped out of existence, either. We also managed to exterminate the Carolina parakeet, a small green-and-yellow bird that ranged from Ohio to New York State and down through the south along the east coast. These pretty birds weren't hunted commercially, but they were relentlessly persecuted as pest birds, even though some farmers valued them because they fed voraciously on the invasive cocklebur, keeping it under control. Their bright feathers also made them popular targets for milliners, and they were often caught and sold as pets. Destruction of their habitat and invasion of their nests by the European honeybee didn't help any, and they also had a species trait that more or less sealed their fate.

Like many flocking birds, they had the habit of gathering around a wounded or dead member of their flock. All you had to do was shoot one, and the others would immediately gather round it protectively, thus making themselves available for slaughter. Apparently, even in the bird world, no good deed will go unpunished. The last members of the species, a couple named Lady Jane and Incas who had been together for thirty-two years, died within a year of each other in 1918.

Beyond shaking your head and muttering what a shame, you might ask so what? We've gotten along fine without moas, dodos, Carolina parakeets, and passenger pigeons. There is a kind of natural attrition of species that allows for such losses without creating a great imbalance. But what might they have added to our existence if they remained? A source of food that we'd still have if we'd shepherded it wisely? A bird that would eat invasive plants so we'd need fewer herbicides? At the least, New York State would have beautiful green and orange parrots flitting around.

Sometimes, too, birds come to our rescue in unexpected ways. Consider, for instance, if we did to gulls what we did to moas. We might not have Utah.

One of the central stories of Mormon settlement in Utah is of a time when their crops were being devastated by a kind of giant, steely jawed cricket. Seeing their food supply destroyed, certain they would starve, and unable to control the hoards of insects, the new community dropped to its knees in the fields and began to pray.

Then, overhead, the sky was suddenly darkened. They looked up to see flocks of gulls thick enough to block the sun. The birds swept down on the insects and ate them all, feeding themselves and saving the starving human settlers, who saw them as angels sent by a merciful God.

The problem is, you don't know ahead of time what you'll lose when you lose a species. A cure for cancer? An important insight into consciousness, both human and bird? A good friend and teacher on a personal level? Imagine, for instance, the pigeon gone from New York City. Urban areas have their own peculiar ecosystem, and certainly the pigeon is part of it. City dwelling peregrine falcons feed on them, so without pigeons, would the falcons also go away? Pigeons themselves eat a lot of street food, so would the city have more garbage without them, and would that lead to an increase in the rat population? With more rats, there would be more fleas, and would that lead to a new episode of the plague, as it did in Europe when the cat population was greatly depleted by Christians because of a presumed association with the devil?

I found no one who could answer that question, and certainly, as a novelist, I may be extending probabilities into strange, improbable realms. But questions like that bear thinking about, because while the absence of moas may or may not matter to humans or planetary balance, caring that birds are protected matters a great deal. To understand why, you can refer to the island of Guam, where almost all the birds are gone.

Following World War Two, warships unknowingly carried a stowaway between islands. The brown tree snake had slithered into their holds on the Admiralty Islands and disembarked at Guam, unnoticed. The birds of Guam had no experience with such predators, and lacking protective behavior, they were easy meals. Consequently, the snake population grew exponentially, while the bird population rapidly declined.

The losses went unnoticed and unmanaged until the early 1960s, when it was clear that several abundant species had disappeared in places where the snakes were most populous. Bird decline continued to spread unchecked, and by the time various species were listed as endangered or threatened through the U.S. Fish and Wildlife service in 1984, they were already gone. Guam lost about 85 percent of its bird population, with nine of its eleven species of native forest-dwelling birds exterminated. Two of them—the Guam rail and the Micronesian kingfisher—are being bred in zoos with hopes that they'll eventually be reintroduced. A few other native species exist in precariously small numbers, and their future is perilous.

Guam has become a living example of Rachel Carson's silent spring, and this has affected other life on the island in a variety of ways. The arboreal brown tree snake likes to climb up power poles and hide inside transformers, where they've caused an enormous increase in power outages, which cost millions of dollars to repair. Without birds, insect life proliferates, and as a result mosquito-borne diseases in humans have increased, and there are reports of wildly abundant populations of spiders on the island. Scientists are also concerned about the effect bird absence is having on seed dispersal. Birds have a role in 60 to 70 percent of tree-seed dispersal, not only scattering the seeds far away from the parent trees, but also removing the seed coats, making germination faster and more certain. In Guam, researchers are seeing a decline in seed dispersal and note that none of the seeds they find have had their coats removed. Tree decline will, of course, further alter the ecosystem, perhaps in even greater ways (sciencedaily.com/releases/2008).

This means that a world without birds is also a world with a reduced tree and plant population, where insects rule. Birds may be small creatures, but they have pretty big jobs.

As global travel increases, the problem of inadvertent new predator introduction becomes more common. The question is, what can be done to prevent such disasters? The brown tree snake is acting its natural role as predator, and we can't just ask it to behave. Introducing another species as a control can be just as dangerous. So what's the solution?

A group called the Global Invasive Species Team, which lists many successful attempts to control or get rid of invasive species, says that the best response is an early one. Perhaps if the brown tree snake had been noticed and dealt with quickly, Guam would still have its birds. But such early intervention requires strong environmental public policy, and a culture that sustains general interest in both larger environmental issues and individual species, on a variety of levels. Citizens groups such as Rich Guthrie's bird counters, individuals such as Ward Stone working in the government, and people like Pete Dubacher who do it on their own are all necessary components of such a culture. So are all the people I spoke with for this book, each one doing their part to educate, inspire, rescue, and heal.

Perhaps species extinction is a natural process and nothing, not even bluebirds, lasts forever. But I will never see a Carolina parakeet, a moa, or a passenger pigeon primarily because of human folly, and I don't think folly is natural. Or at least it shouldn't be, not to humans, whose supposedly clever brains got us to the top of the food chain. Beyond any consideration of environmental balance, the richness of my life is diminished by the absence of these species, just as it would be without blue-birds, eagles, and hummingbirds.

More than two hundred birds are currently on the National Audobon Society's watchlist as in decline or seriously threatened through habitat loss caused by commercial logging, building development, climate change, chemical pollutants such as mer-cury, and more. That makes me more glad than ever for places like the Berkshire Bird Paradise, which gives respite not only to birds, but also to the humans who cherish them.

Pete Dubacher is currently gathering in more birds from areas where their lives are threatened, in hopes of contributing further to the breeding of such species. Still, what continues to amaze me is the way he cares for each bird that comes his way, regard-less of its cultural popularity. In doing so he reminds us that value exists beyond economy, beyond human achievement.

Value lives in the feathers of an owl's wing, and in our capac-ity to recognize that.

 FIFTEEN

Night Owls

What could ever drive a man
To venture out in all this cold? ˙
What could ever be the dream upon his mind,
Or the voice he heard come singing through the snow?
—Jack Hardy, "The Wren"

Eastern screech owls have also been called the common
screech owl, ghost owl, dusk owl, little-eared owl, spirit
owl, little dukelet, Texas screech-owl, whickering owl,
little gray owl, mottled owl, the red owl, the mouse owl,
the cat owl, the shivering owl, and the little horned owl.
—*www.owlpages.com*

Great horned owls have a large repertoire of sounds,
ranging from deep booming hoots to shrill shrieks. The
male's resonant territorial call "hoo-hoo hoooooo hoo-
hoo" can be heard over several miles during a still night.
Both sexes hoot, but males have a lower-pitched voice
than females. They give a growling "krrooo-oo" or
screaming note when attacking intruders. Other sounds
include a "whaaa whaaaaaa-a-a-aarrk" from disturbed
birds, a catlike "MEEE-OWww," barks, hair-raising
shrieks, coos, and beak snapping. Some calls are ventril-
oquial. Most calling occurs from dusk to about midnight
and then again just before dawn.
—*www.owlpages.com*

Midnight, Berkshire Bird Paradise

I DRAG MYSELF out of my foofy bed with reluctance, and wonder how Pete manages to do this so often, in much worse weather. Though I often write through the night, to my mind it's one thing to stay up all night when you're deep in a novel that overrides any fatigue. It's another to climb out of a warm bed in order to face a cold, damp night.

When I creep outside, the sanctuary is dark. Really dark. There's no ambient light from cities here, so I bring a flashlight, but when I flick it on the geese raise a fuss, like overexcited children who think the party's just started. It's a very loud fuss, so in the interest of peace, I click the flashlight off. The geese pretty quickly settle down. I live in the country, with no streetlights, so I know enough to wait for my eyes to adjust.

As I stand in the dark, listening to the sibilant mutterings of waterfowls, I think of a story Bill Danielson told me. He had a friend visiting from the city, and when they went out onto his deck at night she said, "Wow. At night, it's, like, *dark* out." It made her nervous, he said, as if she was waiting for a bear or a monster to leap out of the woods at her. She didn't realize that in our neighborhood it's so quiet at night you'd hear anything long before you saw it.

The same is true of the sanctuary. Beyond the quiet night bird sounds, there's no traffic, no blaring radios, nothing at all between you and the wind. Pete told me earlier that he's thinking of building a kind of hermitage for people who want to come and stay over to be in the silence. I told him I thought it would be a good idea. A place where you could hear yourself think.

The soft whining of the wheelbarrow to my right signals me that Pete is out stoking one of the stoves, but I'm not going to look for him. If he's like me, this is not the time to be sociable, or even verbal. Night is for contemplation, and prayer that takes the form of work, whether that's writing or hauling wood.

I walk around slowly, carefully, peering into various aviaries. The birds are mostly asleep. I stop at the raven house and take a look inside. The buzzards are gathered in their Play Cave. The ravens and crows are gathered in small clusters, cuddling. One of them turns and peers at me, then tucks a beak back into a friend's wing.

"That's so cute," I whisper at them. It really is. One doesn't normally think of ravens and crows as cuddlers. Seeing them this way creates a whole new impression.

I make my way slowly toward the owl houses, thinking that they're probably awake, maybe even active. When I get there and look inside the owls stare at me briefly, then turn away. I'm not interesting, either as predator or prey. I sit on one of the nearby benches and feel the night.

Owls hold a special place in mythology the world over. Perhaps because of their golden stares, those eyes that seem to look right through you. Or perhaps because they're elusive night creatures, each sighting seems heavy with portent. Legend in Afghanistan says that the owl gave man flint and iron to make fire—in exchange, man gave the owl his feathers. In Algeria, if you place the right eye of an eagle owl in the hand of a sleeping woman, she will tell all. Australian aborigines believe owls represent the souls of men and owls the souls of women. Owls are therefore sacred, because your sister is an owl—and the owl is your sister.

Pete has great horned owls, barn owls, a screech owl—something I always expected to be large but which is actually diminutive—and barred owls, many of which are from the Hudson Valley Raptor Center. These latter are extending their range in the west, and that's been a problem, since they're competing with spotted owls, who are suffering a decline due to habitat loss. But in our area I often hear them at night, calling out, "Who cooks for you?" That's how their call is described in the bird books, and in fact, it does sound like they're saying that. When I hear them in my yard, I always make my husband answer the question.

Once I'm settled by the owl aviary, the soft sound of hooting begins, an eerie, mournful sound. Then, a more distant chorus of hooting. A quiet hoo-hoo hoooooo hoo-hoo from the local great horned owls, the wild relatives calling back from the woods.

Hoo hoo, Pete's owls say. A pause, and hoo-hoo, someone in the woods answers. It's a conversation, and I am a foreign eavesdropper who wishes she knew the language.

What they say is a song of secrets that we humans sometimes long to share. It's a private tongue, expressing an experience of the world that's different from ours, in many ways, and perhaps in some ways the same. Cold is cold, hunger is hunger, no matter how you voice it.

But that longing to understand, to meet a different consciousness and learn from it, remains. A few years ago, I was working on a fantasy novel where the characters were being led on their quest by an owl. It was winter as I was working that part out, and one night I came home very late from a solstice performance I'd been at. The performers were wonderful, the event itself all you could ask for in terms of magic and mystery to celebrate the longest night.

I drove up the long, winding hill to my home at about 1:00 A.M., and as I turned one of the curves it seemed that suddenly some of the snow to my right reshaped itself and lifted off. I stared at it, and then realized it was a very large white owl, and it was flying toward me. It stared at me, and I had that wonderful moment of meeting what is wild, looking it in the eye. You are kin after all, it says. You are family to the planet, to its creatures. Too surprised to react, I just kept driving, and the owl slid into the airspace in front of my car, flying in front of me directly over my hood, leading me all the way home.

When I pulled into my driveway it flew off. I stopped my car and sat there, still stunned. I am kin to what is wild. We are family. Sometimes, we're even friends, leading each other home.

As part of my research for this book, I asked many people I know why they get a thrill from interactions with wild birds or animals. At first they'd just say, "Well, it's a cool thing," or, "It's great to see them." But why, I wanted to know. What in particular do they feel in those moments, and why does it matter to them? Meeting an owl or a deer won't pay the bills or solve your love life problems. So what exactly does it do?

My husband said, "It's about freedom. They're so free, when you meet one, you remember what freedom is. You feel it again." One of my students said, "It's a feeling of belonging. Like we belong to something much larger than us." And my son said,

"When you're out walking and a bird or a deer suddenly appears in front you, you feel chosen. They didn't have to come out to see you, but they did. They chose you."

For me, besides the sense of family and connection, the experience is a broadening of my consciousness, a moment to see the world from the eyes of another species. When I see my dog sniff in the woods, I know she experiences the world through a different medium, and I can try to imagine what that's like. When an owl looks in my eyes, I can wonder what she sees that I do not.

Your answer may be totally different from any of these. The many answers to my question indicate that interaction with birds and other nonhuman creatures is as varied as the human experience. If you're cynical, you can see that as projection. Maybe my husband says freedom because he's extremely responsible, and sometimes longs for freedom. My student said belonging because she feels alone, just a cog in the incomprehensible wheel of the world. My son said chosen because he wants to believe in the dream that comes naturally to an only child—that of being special, being chosen.

"If that's the case, I don't want to know," my husband says about that. "I don't want to ruin the experience."

Personally, I don't think any of the answers grow from dysfunction. Instead, I think they come from our best human urge to broaden our lives, deepen our empathy and our understanding. What we lack, we yearn to know more about. That's not a bad thing.

In the quiet night, I understand that Pete and his family get to experience some of this every day. They live in the place where wild and domestic meet, an interstitial space, like the middle of the night, where both are possible, and both can learn from each other, no matter what language is used. For me, that's another piece in the puzzle of why anyone would choose to work so hard, giving up much of what we define as success in America in the twenty-first century. He doesn't have fancy cars or a big house, he goes out to dinner maybe once a year, and counts decades between vacations. But every day, he has at least a little magic. Communication with foreign consciousness, belonging to something bigger, knowing his work is necessary for these lives he nurtures, a reminder of what's essential in life rather than arbitrary. That's all the good stuff, really.

When I feel I've learned enough, I walk my chilled body back to my warm and foofy bed, wondering mostly what Pete's Dad will be cooking for breakfast.

 SIXTEEN

What It Is about Pigeons

The flutter of blue pigeon's wings
Under a river bridge
Hunting a clean dry arch,
A corner for a sleep—
This flutters here in a woman's hand.
A singing sleep cry,
A drunken poignant two lines of song,
Somebody looking clean into yesterday
And remembering, or looking clean into
To-morrow, and reading,—
This sings here as a woman's sleep cry sings.
Pigeon friend of mine,
Fly on, sing on.

                    —*Carl Sandburg, "Pigeon"*

8 A.M., Berkshire Bird Paradise
PANCAKES. Really good pancakes, with bacon and yummy coffee. That's what William makes for breakfast.

As I stumble downstairs the sun makes itself known with thin and scratchy lines of yellow scraping through what is primarily a grey sky. At the ragtail end of October, the weather here in the foothills of the Berkshires is unpredictable. You could get heavy frost or even snow, bone-biting damp and rain, or t-shirt weather. In fact, while the average low temperature for October is 39 degrees, and the average high is 60, the record high temperature is 91 degrees, set in 1941, and the record low is 16 degrees, set in 1969.

Today, we'll get drizzle that gnaws rather than bites, and temperatures in the high forties. And regardless, the work will go on. I sneak outside to see what's happening. At this time of day, the residents are greeting the day. A rooster crows. The sandhill cranes clack and hoot. The geese and crows honk and caw, respectively. It's a cross between heavy metal and free-form jazz, all of it underscored by the more baroque cooings of 150 pigeons, the low, complex song of the East African crowned cranes, the drumming of the emus and the auditorium-strength conversation of the exotic birds.

Morning at the Berkshire Bird Paradise is a multitextural experience of sound. Grating, soothing, silky, jagged, piercing, blunt, nubby, fluffy all at once. Those whose morning begins with the alarm or the radio or the passage of morning traffic might find it disturbing because it's so layered, so unexpected. And even if you can't translate the sound to human tongue, it has the feel of speech. It's not technology talking. It's living creatures.

As I'm walking around, I see Betty Ann, just driving off, on her way to work. She rolls down her car window and smiles at me, "Good morning. How are you?"

"Good. I'm good."

"I hope you slept well?"

"Yes, I did. But I got up in the night to walk around."

Her face lets go of its politeness and takes on the knowing look of two people who share mysteries. "It's special, right?" she notes.

"It sure is," I agree.

"I'm glad you went out," she says.

"So am I," I tell her.

She drives away, and I head back to the kitchen where Christine is fussing over plates at the table, and William is busy at the stove. I smell bacon in the air. I know better than to ask if I can help.

"I have hotcakes for you," William says quietly.

"You like hotcakes?" Christine chirps. "Yes? Sit. Sit. Coffee?"

"Yes. Coffee," I agree.

I sit at the table and William brings me three perfectly formed and cooked pancakes, which I dive into, hungry as everything

else that lives here, and just as well fed. By the time I'm content-
edly sipping my coffee, Pete comes bustling in.

"Good morning," he says. "Sleep okay?"

"I got up and listened to the owls."

"Oh yeah? I thought I heard someone walking around. How
was it?"

"Lovely. They talk to teach other—yours and the wild ones."

"They sure do. We got some help coming today. A guy named
Alex and a kid from Cobleskill. A student. They'll be here a little
later."

"That's good," I say. "Anything else on the agenda?"

"The usual. I'm going out to the pigeons first."

That, I have to see. Pete has a thing about pigeons. He's
taking in a variety of exotic pigeons from around the world, but
he also has his almost two hundred pigeons that were brought to
him from pigeon rescue groups, primarily in New York City. I
trail out after him to the pigeon house, a large aviary covered in
green canvas. From the outside, it's one giant coo, a marshmallow
sound that soothes.

When we enter, it's the same, but the cooers are in motion.
Two hundred pairs of wings flutter up at our entrance, and a soft
dust gives everything a filtered look. It's angelic, in fact. Heav-
enly. Suddenly, I understand why these birds were so often used
in Christian imagery.

Pete, down to earth, gets busy cleaning out basins of water. "I
gotta do this two or three times a day. Pigeons take a lot of baths."

He doesn't have to prove his point. As soon as he changes the
water, a puff of pigeons scoot over and begin bathing, fluffing
their wings, clearly enjoying the water immensely.

"Most people say they're dirty," I note.

"People say all kinds of things about pigeons," Pete says, and
shakes his head.

He's right. Some people call them rats with wings. Some call
them rock doves. Some see them as the scourge of the city, and
some as the last remaining link that city dwellers have with the
natural world. However you view them, they've been around a
long time, and a part of human life for as long as there have been
humans.

Pigeon is a French translation of the English word *dove*, and technically all pigeons are doves. They are, in some ways, the bird version of dogs, domesticated by humans shortly after dogs were, and used for their talents in speedy, long distance flight. In his book *Pigeons*, Andrew Blechman notes that a pigeon delivered the results of the first Olympics in 776 B.C.E. and brought news of Napoleon's defeat 2,500 years later. Nearly a million pigeons served in both World Wars, saving thousands of soldier's lives. They're mentioned in Mesopotamian cuneiform tablets and Egyptian hieroglyphics. Egyptians used them to fly in the four directions, announcing the ascension of a new Pharoah, and ancient sailors used them for their capacity to find land.

Pigeon courier was by far the swiftest form of communication for a long time, with these birds delivering their messages in as many hours as it took a horse and rider days. Built for speed and endurance, they've been clocked at up to 110 miles per hour. Homing pigeons routinely fly over five hundred miles in a single day at speeds exceeding sixty miles per hour, without stopping for food or water. And they can do all this on about an ounce of bird seed a day.

They are, in fact, pretty special birds. Even today they're used as competitors in races that pay more than—um—pigeon feed. The Bronx based Main Event pigeon race offer a $15,000 prize, not to mention the tens of thousands to be made in bets.

Cornell University also has an interest in them, and runs a program called Project Pigeon, which focuses on pigeon colors. Cornell educator Karen Purcell says what's interesting about pigeon colors is that they have so many. In general, it's best to blend in with the crowd if you're a prey animal, since predators look for differences as visual cues of what animal to hunt. Pigeons, a domesticated bird gone feral, have maintained their color differences, and ornithologists still wonder why that's so.

But Pete's interest in pigeons isn't about color or racing potential. For him, they're birds who need homes, and he's got the only facility willing to take them in on this scale. Some time ago, his sanctuary came to the attention of a group of people in New York City who rescue pigeons. Pigeons starting coming his way from people like Beverly Mastropolos, wife of Frank Mastropolos, who produces the show 20/20. People like Tootie Wittmer, a former Broadway costume designer. People like Alice Husum, who spent $800 to get a city pigeon's leg fixed, then brought it to Pete's place to live when she couldn't keep it comfortably. She still comes to visit her ward.

And people like Dan Woldin, owner/operator of Madison Media in New York City. He worked with animals when he was young, but then he became financially ambitious, and decided to start his own media and marketing business. That proved successful, but there was part of him that wanted to participate in the world in different ways. He wanted to do something meaningful.

"Then," he told me, "I was walking home one day. It was snowing out, cold. I saw a pigeon stumbling around on the street. It was clearly sick, probably dying. I thought, 'how sad,' and I moved on."

But when he got into his warm apartment the pigeon stayed on his mind. He thought it should at least be comfortable in its last hours, so he got a towel and went out and wrapped the pigeon up, and put it in a bush. When he was inside again, he realized that it was silly to leave it out when he had a nice warm apartment, so he went back out, found it, and brought it in.

Though ailing, the pigeon continued to stay alive, so he looked up pigeons on the internet, and found a pigeon rescue website. "I wrote my problem on their message board, and the system put me in a chatroom. They said I could bring the bird to Animal General, a veterinarian practice that has vets who care for injured pigeons. They have licensed rehabilitators, a blood lab, x-ray, and a list of rehabilitators and people who foster pigeons. The goal is to get them well enough to be released into a flock that gets food and water every day."

As a result the pigeon, named Pidge, was saved. Pidge stayed with Dan, who was working from his home at the time. Pidge would stay at his desk and eventually, mimicking Dan, would peck at his computer keys. When Pidge started getting feisty, Dan knew it was time to release it. He let Pidge fly off a neighbor's balcony, and the bird often returned to that spot, perching there and watching the neighbor as he worked at his computer, perhaps hoping to get another peck or two in.

After this, Dan was hooked. He kept taking in pigeons, until he had about a dozen living in his apartment. They had their own room, and a house all their own within the room. Two of them, Tom and Dick, came to him as babies and were hand raised. He didn't think they'd fare well if they were released into the wild, but he was spending more and more time on pigeons and less and less on his own business. It was becoming a problem.

Fortunately, a woman who works at Animal General had heard about the Berkshire Bird Paradise, where Pete Dubacher would take a pigeon for a $250 donation, and feed it and house it for the rest of its natural life, which could be fifteen more years. She hadn't actually seen the place and was curious about it, so Dan was sent upstate to find out what he could, and bring some pigeons to Pete if it all checked out.

"All the way there, I kept thinking bad things about the place," Dan told me. "I was suspicious, you know? I thought Pete was using the pigeons as feed for the predator birds, because who'd be crazy enough to take in pigeons for that little money?"

When he arrived, he took the tour with Pete, but then he hemmed and hawed about leaving the birds. "Pete said let's take a walk, and we did. We talked about Pete's time in the army, and how that left him with the feeling of wanting to use his life to help what was in pain rather than cause more pain. He brought me inside the pigeon house, and I noticed that they were fed really good food. I mean, really good. Even better than I used. Pete had cedar chips on the aviary ground, and when it got soiled, he'd sell it for fertilizer. He let the pigeons walk on his head, and he seemed to know them all. I realized that he was the real deal, and I left the birds with him."

Some time passed, and Dan decided to go check on his birds, to make sure they hadn't become eagle food. He didn't give Pete much notice. Just called and said he was on his way. "I kind of wanted to check up on him," Dan admits. "But Pete just said, 'I'd love to see you. Come on out.'"

When he arrived Pete brought him into the aviary that now houses about one hundred and fifty pigeons. He pointed to one. "That's Tom, right there. See him looking at you?"

"I was so surprised—first that he knew which one was Tom, and then to actually see him. I just shouted, 'My god—Tom' And he flew right over and landed on my shoulder, jumped on my head, and started pecking."

By then, Dan admits, the tears were streaming down his face. And finally, he believed that Pete was who he claimed to be, doing what he claimed to do. He started to bring more birds to the sanctuary after that. And he had a kind of epiphany of his own. It occurred to him that if he made a lot of money, he could actually do much more to help birds than he did by trying to rehab them. He stopped fostering birds, focused on his business, and used his money to good purpose, contributing more to Pete's efforts, and using his resources to support the New York City efforts in pigeon rescue.

For instance, when the pigeon rescue website gets notice that a pigeon's in trouble—as in, "pigeon down on fourth street, near dumpster"—if the reporting person can't or won't bring it over to Animal General, he has a list of rescuers who will. For this service, he pays them $100.

"A lot of these people are either underemployed, or struggling with physical or mental illness, or for other reasons not functional in the world," he says. "The money helps them as well as the birds, and it gives them a sense of purpose. So everybody wins."

He also buys three hundred pounds of bird seed every two weeks, and he and others—including his mother—spread it around every day to feed the birds. Sometimes they catch flak, but more often he's surprised at how nice people are.

One day as he was scattering seed he saw two older women, nicely dressed, clearly upper class, approaching him. Walking slightly behind them was a Hispanic man in a maintenance uniform. The two women passed by without a word, but the Hispanic man kept his eye on Dan, and was approaching with the clear intent of saying something. Dan fully expected him to say something nasty. Instead, he said, "I just want to tell you, I think it's wonderful, what you're doing."

Dan, ready for an argument, was relieved. "Then the guy told me that the two women who walked by called me a pig. They said I was the reason there were pigeon problems in the city. So

you never know who's going to be nice, and who'll give you a
hard time." To avoid trouble, he took to hiding the seed in bags
up his sleeve, letting it fall out as he walked, like a prisoner getting rid of dirt from the tunnel he was digging for escape.

"One woman told me that I was responsible for the rat problem in the city, because rats would eat the leftover seed. But I'll
tell you what, I can put out seed in the morning, and it's gone
before noon. The birds get to it fast. The rats never have a
chance. So I told her, 'you're the cause of rat problems, when you
throw out rotten tomatoes and meat.'"

Clearly, this makes him angry. "Some of these people say animals and birds have no souls. How dare they pretend to know
that? I look at animals and I think they're exactly like me. They
have pain and hunger. They have their lives."

Dan spends both time and money to care for these little souls,
and I couldn't help but wonder what he got out of it. When I
asked him that, he laughed.

"I'll tell you what, I get a parking space right in front of the
building wherever I go. Doesn't matter how crowded the streets
are, what time it is. That space is waiting for me. I expect it to be
there."

"So the pigeons are your parking angels?"

"Yeah. You might say that."

That was the end of the conversation, but later he called me
back. He'd been thinking more about my question, and had
another answer.

"People walk along in their day, connected to iPods and cell-
phones, caught up in all our stupid human crap," he said. "Then
they come across an injured animal or bird, and they have a
choice. A real, immediate choice. They can stop and salvage this
little life, or move on. A lot of people, including myself, suddenly
realize they can do something positive about the destiny of this
particular existence, and they feel the power of that. Men often
think they have power when they have a gun, but a moment like
that makes them see that the real power is in rescue. That's what
firefighters do. Someone rushing into a burning building is exercising power. Someone rescuing a bird is exercising power. It's a
place we don't often get—a place where we can be immediately

PETE AND TOM THE PIGEON.

effective. A place to exercise the human capacity for compassion, and that's our real power."

Dan's pigeon Tom is still with Pete, along with many pigeon friends.

"I tell you what," Pete says. "These pigeons are a big part of keeping this place afloat. The people who bring them are very generous."

That, I think, is a kindness returned, just like in the old folk-tales.

 SEVENTEEN

Visitors

Most bird records are set on the wing; the emu can boast a rather unusual record—as the world's furthest walking bird. It cannot fly, so must walk during its migrations. The pattern of rainy and dry seasons in Australia forces the emu to follow rain clouds in search of water. Emus are believed to respond to the low frequency sound of raindrops hitting the ground. Nevertheless they often have to walk as far as 320 miles following the rain clouds.

—www.pbs.org/lifeofbirds/champions/index.html

10 A.M., Berkshire Bird Paradise.
"DON'T YOU JUST love birds?" Stephanie asks, waving her arms with enthusiasm. "Wow. What a place."

Stephanie is a first-year student at SUNY Cobleskill's Fisheries and Wildlife program. She's enthusiastic, full of energy, ready to learn everything. Dressed for work instead of fashion, ready with her notebook and her phone camera, she's here to do research for a class presentation. It's her first time here, and her father has come along to see the place, as well as to spend time with his only daughter, whose first year at college has been a big transition for him.

Pete regularly gets volunteers from both Cobleskill and Massachusets College of Liberal Arts (MCLA). Some visit for a day, and some take on longer internships. Stephanie, originally from the Rochester area, is snapping photos of the African cranes when Pete comes by and introduces himself.

They shake hands, and she beams up at him with something like awe. "Wow," she says. "You do all this? This is great."

He rubs at the back of his neck, shrugs it off. "We like it," he says. "I tell you what, I've got another helper coming—Alex. Maybe you can walk around with Barbara until he gets here, and then he'll put you to work. After that I'll find you and we can talk for a while. How's that sound?"

"Sounds good to me," I say.

Pete takes off and I start Stephanie and her father down one of the mazelike paths, moving toward the duck pond. Stephanie continues taking pictures, chattering animatedly as we go. "Is that a wood duck?" she points at one. "Really? A wood duck?"

"I think it's Woody the wood duck," I say, and tell her the story, which she says is cool.

"I have to get a picture of you," she says. "A real writer. Do you read Stephanie Meyers? I *love* her."

Writers get asked that kind of thing a lot, and there isn't much to say about it. I smile, and give my stock answer, that it's hard for me to find time to read something I didn't write. We move on to an aviary full of hawks from the Hudson Valley Raptor Center, and Stephanie studies them, takes some notes.

Her father trails after her, peering at the birds with her. He's a quiet man, about my age, and his jeans and jacket look fit in here. I get the impression of a liberal, someone who has his own interests in the environment. I also get the impression of someone like the other men I've met in connection with this book—a man who's been a good and loving father to his daughter.

When I join him and Stephanie at the hawk house, the birds are staring at us with their intense, raptor eyes. Her father turns to me. "This is something else. It's so great to get this close to the birds. You can really get a feel for what they're like."

"It does. You share Stephanie's wildlife interests?"

He smiles. "Maybe not quite as much. She's got a lot of enthusiasm. But I like places where you can really interact with the animals. My brother lives in Hilo—Hawaii—and every year we'd go there, visit the zoo. It's like this—not a huge place, and you can get close to the animals. They had an aviary, with all the birds flying around. Stephanie loved it. So do I."

We move on to the eagles, and Stephanie takes more notes, more pictures. She's putting together a PowerPoint for her presentation, and is very excited about the eagle stories that are posted in front of the cages. As she's working, we get company—a lanky, blonde teenage boy, who approaches and speaks.

"Pete said I should find you," he says quietly. "I'm Alex."

"Great. I'm Barbara—here writing about the place. This is Stephanie and her father, here to help. So what's on the agenda?"

Alex stares at me, frowning a little.

"What's your work for today?" I try.

"Clean the cages, move some wood, feed the emus," he says, remaining laconic.

We move off, Stephanie already chatting to him at a rapid rate as we make our way to the tropical bird house.

The sharply musty scent of feathers is what you notice first here. That, and the volume. Squeaks and squawks, coos and small cackles surround you. Conversation is constant, and sometimes overwhelming. Human conversation takes a back seat, unless you want to shout "What?" a lot. The birds here are macaws, parrots, finches, cockatiels and cockatoos. Some were abandoned, and some had owners who died or moved and could no longer house them. Some proved too noisy for their apartment dwellings, or too unmanageable for their owners.

Pete has about fifty tropicals, some here for more than twenty years. And he continues to get more. Just recently he had a call from a woman in Delmar who's going into assisted living, and has three ring-necked doves she couldn't bring with her. They'll all take up residence in Paradise.

He's had some interesting ones. There was Pancho, an Amazon parrot brought in by a German woman who was moving to Hawaii, where the rules about what you can and can't bring to the islands are strict. Pancho, like his human, was bilingual, speaking both German and English. Later, Pete acquired another Amazon parrot who speaks Spanish and English.

One of the reasons an owner might prefer to bring them here is that this setting gives them a stable environment, instead of going from owner to owner as they might if they were sold or given away. And here these social birds can vocalize with each other, provide company for each other. In this way they're constantly stimulated, and pretty happy about it from the sounds of things. Though he can't currently let them fly because they're chewing birds who might get into wires, they have large cages and ample opportunity to interact.

Pete doesn't adopt them out, but instead signs on to keep all of them for life unless the original owners are able to take them back through a change in circumstance. He does this both for previous owners who still come back to visit their birds, and to avoid unscrupulous people who say they'll adopt, then turn around and sell them.

They're not the easiest birds to care for, either. They need heat and plenty of it, so the temperature in their house never goes below 65 degrees. It's a goodly collection of cockatoos, cockatiels, macaws, and various parrots. And they make a lot of noise. And they poop. A lot.

Alex and Stephanie get busy with cleaning up after them, removing cage trays, dumping old contents, wiping down surfaces and putting in new bedding. Water and food holders are cleaned and filled. Small mountains of bird droppings are scraped away.

"How come you work here?" I shout at Alex above the din.

He looks at me like I'm a little weird. "Because I get paid?" he says, barely loud enough for me to hear.

"You'd get paid at Pizza Hut, too," I note.

This earns me a small smile. "My dad worked here. It's a good place. Gets noisy, though."

"Yeah," I shout, and then I give up on talking. Human conversation is just too much effort. As Christine said, this place belongs to the birds. They are, perhaps, telling each other all about us, maybe excited, or maybe giving instructions on how they want their cages cleaned. Exotic birds, whose natural homes are rainforests with thick canopies of trees, have voices that were made to carry long distances, out in the open. In this closed space, with so much to talk about, they're a blending of cacophonies.

Even so, individual voices separate themselves as you approach individual cages. I'm wiping a cockatoo cage when I hear a vague, very human muttering above me.

I look up, and the cockatoo flares his head feathers, making himself impressive. "Is that you?" I ask.

He ducks his head, turns shyly away. I go back to wiping, and again hear the muttering, a soft current of sound under all the squawks.

"It *is* you," I say.

This time he admits it, walking ponderously up the bars of the cage and muttering his affirmation.

"You'll have to speak up, or something," I suggest.

More muttering. This time I'm convinced it's an answer. Something like, "Well, mutter mutter, you know I don't like to talk up very loud, no, no, so rude to do that, not really the thing, you know, not at all, mutter mutter."

It's so close to human speech that I'm compelled to move closer, waiting to for the words that will surely become fully comprehensible if I just listen a little harder. When I do, a nearby parrot gives out some piercing squawks, and the cockatoo mutters himself to the back of his cage and says no more.

When the exotics are tended, Alex moves on to shifting wood, and Stephanie goes along. Her father and I take a walk back to the pond, where the ducks, geese, and swans are paddling about in the water, honking quietly to each other, preening feathers.

Some geese raise their voices, craning their necks at each other, in vehement discussion about some fine bird point that eludes our perception. Once when I was here, two geese got in a fight. Pete yelled, "Hey!" and picked one up by the neck, holding it close. "That's enough," he said firmly. The goose honked quietly at him, but when he was released, he smoothed his feathers and stayed out of trouble. I'd seen episodes like that on the *Dog Whisperer*, but that was the first time I saw a goose pack-leader in action.

Stephanie's father sighs. "This is my daughter's first year at school," he says.

"Is she your only?" I ask, and he nods.

"That's tough," I say sympathetically. My son is an only. I remember the adjustment I had when he went away to school.

"It is. A lot tougher than I thought it would be. I just miss her."

Fathers and daughters. I think of Pete's concern for his own daughter, the totem pole he carved for her. I think of Ward Stone and the art he made for his deceased daughter, the love he has for his living daughter. I wonder if there's some connection between men who value wildlife and also love their daughters. I think of my own father, who made us read Rachel Carson and taught us to pick up litter along the side of the road. Do men who love the earth teach their daughters well, or do men who love their daughters also learn to love the earth in a different way? Or maybe it's both, an intertwined learning.

"She seems to like it," I note.

"She's having a great time. It's a good program."

Cobleskill's curriculum is very hands-on. Kevin Burner, who teaches Wildlife Management and Wildlife Techniques classes at Cobleskill, requires students in his classes to do an independent study or community service. Quite a few of them end up fulfilling those requirements here, at the Berkshire Bird Paradise, and Kevin says they universally love it.

"Even if they're spreading hay in the birdhouses, they're excited by Peter's attitude and devotion," he told me, "especially when they realize it's pretty much a one-man show, and he must just marginally survive doing it, but he has the passion. They go out of their way to help him, knowing they can make a difference."

Kevin himself is a bluebird expert. When I asked him what kind of food I should put out to draw more bluebirds to my place, he told me he'd done an experiment to find out what they eat in the winter. He found their winter roosts, and he collected their droppings. He took his collection home, and he germinated it to see what would grow.

Yes. That's right. He planted bird poop.

If you think about it, it's a simple and brilliant solution, since birds are nature's seed dispersers, their droppings full of what they eat. Most of it, he told me, was sumac. The next favorite winter food was poison ivy berries. Go figure.

Kevin was always interested in wildlife. At the age of eight he set up his own blind and put bird seed out so he could see the birds up close. They would be within a foot of him, and that closeness fascinated him. Now, he sends students to Pete so they, too, can get close to the birds.

Lately he's worried about how the bird sanctuary will fare in troubled economic times. "To lose Pete would be disastrous," he said. "He has such a tremendous amount of knowledge. And my students come back from his place so excited. He's a living example of what I tell them—that they should work at something they have a passion for, something that makes the world a better place."

Regardless of human worries or enthusiasms, the ducks and geese continue their preening routine, and in a little while, Stephanie returns, this time with Pete.

"Alex is going to feed the emus," Pete tells us. "You can go help if you want."

I'm a big fan of the emus, so I'm up for it. Before we go, Stephanie takes a few pictures of me and Pete, and then turns her enthusiastic smile to Pete. "This is so great," she says. "Are the birds affectionate?"

Pete knits his brow. "Well, not really. I mean, they recognize me. I'm the guy that brings the rats, right? But I don't encourage them to be affectionate. They're wild, and we want them to stay that way. Especially the chicks. If they imprint on humans we can't release them."

Stephanie's father sighs at this. Stephanie takes a moment to absorb it. There's a gap between our Disney fantasies of animal friends, and the reality of creatures who are, as Pete says, wild, even when they've got a permanent home with humans. Right now her father understands the need to love and let go. Stephanie will, too, when she has children of her own, and Pete and the birds will be added to her list of teachers for this lesson.

In the meantime, Pete goes his own way, and I go with Stephanie and her father to see the most Disney-like birds here. The emus.

We find Alex at the big boxes of produce lined up under a tarp near the house. He's already picking through them, tossing the rotting ones, taking any labels or tags off the good ones before tossing them into a wheelbarrow. Stephanie and I pitch in to help.

EMUS ARE CURIOUS BIRDS, IN EVERY SENSE OF THE PHRASE.

THE FALLOW DEER.

"They don't get chopped or anything?" I ask.

"No. Just toss 'em in," he says.

He adds some huge bags of feed to the top of the load, and we head toward the back part of the sanctuary, to the fenced in area where the emus, the fallow deer, and an ostrich roam. The fallow deer are from the Williamstown estate that once belonged to Prentiss Hall. When they were no longer wanted there, they found a home with Pete, who manages their population by separating male from female during breeding season. And he doesn't eat any of them, though I'd imagine his father is tempted now and again.

The ostrich belonged to a woman who wanted one as a conversation piece, then found they needed more than talk. The emus came here in the early 1990s, and have had an important impact on the sanctuary, and on Pete's life philosophy.

In 1991 Pete had a pair of emus who produced seven emu babies. In 1992, a man showed up at the sanctuary and asked if he'd sell them. Pete was reluctant, and the man said, "Well, if you want to sell let me know, because you can make some money. They've gone up in value."

Pete decided not to, but another man called and offered $3,000 a piece, without even seeing them. Pete sold them, keeping two, who produced more babies. Soon after he was offered $35,000 for four. He sold, and put the money he'd earned back into the sanctuary.

"People were throwing money at emus the way they did at the internet, or real estate. It was amazing. Then, by 1994, they were worthless. People were dumping them, leaving them along the side of the road."

Now he has fifteen emus, mostly dumped when, as Pete says, the emu bubble burst. "That's my password, now," he laughs. "When I say something's just an emu bubble, that's what I mean."

Those bubbles may grow and burst, but Pete still has his first two Emus, along with about a dozen others. We wheel our load toward the gate, where a cluster are already gathered, anticipating lunch. They consider us with placid interest as we go inside, some of them drumming softly.

They're beautiful birds, about six feet tall, with long soft feathers that look like dried fern leaves when they fall. Their necks are marked with pale flourescent blue, a startling color among the muted brown and grey feathers.

It's possible that I'm fond of them because they dispel our cultural myths that see males as amorous wanderers, while females demand fidelity. Emus aren't like that at all. Once the female lays her eggs, she goes blithely off seeking other male partners, while the male sits on the eggs. In a good season, the female might nest three times. And they all eat a lot.

Alex brings four huge bags of feed to the feeding trough, breaks them open and dumps it in. The emus don't wait to be invited, but gather around immediately and dive in.

We leave them to it, and help Alex bring the produce outside, where we begin scattering it around. Some of the emus follow us, along with the ostrich. I wonder how they'll manage whole tomatoes and peppers and more, but quickly the ostrich grabs a banana in its beak and swallows it whole. We can clearly see the banana's outline as it proceeds down the Ostrich's throat.

AN ALL-YOU-CAN-EAT BUFFET FOR EMUS.

"Cool," Stephanie murmurs.

"Very cool," I agree. I remember a similar scene from the movie Fantasia. Apparently not all Disney portrayals of birds are wishful thinking.

I glance over at Stephanie's face. Her expression is a mix of wonder and delight. "It's just like Fantasia," she murmurs.

"That's what I was thinking," I reply.

And I realize that for young people like Stephanie, for all the others who visit here, what everyone says about the place is right. It provides not only a haven for birds, but also a sanctuary for young minds and young imaginings, showing both the reality and the magic of wild birds in a very up-close setting.

It's a place where new thoughts, new ideas, new wonder, can grow and be born. And that, it seems, is something we need now more than ever.

EIGHTEEN

The Next Generation

A bird doesn't sing because it has an answer, it sings because it has a song.

—*Maya Angelou*

WHEN I WAS growing up, it was a rare day that we didn't play outside. In the summer, we were only inside long enough to eat breakfast, and then mothers up and down the block would shoo their children out the door. "Go play," they'd say, and we did.

Without structured activities, lessons, or supervision, we roamed the streets with the off-leash dogs, exploring local gullies and woods where we built makeshift forts and staged imaginary adventures, or playing kickball in someone's yard, or picking wild berries from brambles at the back of empty lots.

We'd return home, full of dirt and berries, and go out again at dark to catch fireflies.

When my son was growing up, he and his friends did the same. My friend Angela, whose children are a little younger than my son, also had that chance. She told me that one year her daughters rescued a baby robin, which they named Fluffy. They fed it chunks of crushed up worms. She admits it was a little disgusting, becoming so intimately aware of the feeding habits of birds, but the interaction gave them a whole different relationship with birds, one that was both more realistic, and more empathetic.

After a while, they took Fluffy outside and pointed to worms, saying, "See that? Eat it!" And he did. Eventually, he flew away, and the girls were sad to see him go, but understood that everything has to live where and how it's best suited. And they never forgot the event. They continued to be more observant of birds.

The next spring, when a flock of robins showed up in the yard, Angela's daughter called to her excitedly, "Mommy, Mommy, Fluffy's back. And he brought *friends!*"

Sadly, both grade-school teachers and my college students tell me this kind of lifestyle, this kind of interaction, is becoming increasingly rare. Safety fears, organized activities, more homework, greater pressures on working families, and new technologies all combine to keep young people from exploring their own natural worlds with the freedom we had when we were young.

Bird Educator Beth Bidwell is just one of the people who is concerned for what this means to this generation's relationship with the environment. She's a former bird rehabber, now executive director of the Wildlife Institute of Eastern New York. She brings her wild birds to schools and museums more than three hundred times a year to teach people about birds, and to simply give them an opportunity to get interested in the wild.

"Kids don't have time to explore the way we did," she notes. "They have more homework, more soccer practice and dance classes and TV and video games. So after we spend time with the birds, I'll give them homework. Turn off your TV, your iPod, your Xbox and Wii and computer—the list goes on and on, and they look more horrified with every piece of technology I mention. When I'm done, I tell them to go outside and look around!"

She laughs as she says it, but she means it seriously, and she says it helps. "I'll see the same kids the following year and they'll tell me, 'I did my homework, and I saw this bird.' It's my job to help open their eyes, so they're observing their surroundings. Just seeing your environment is the start of realizing you're part of it. You belong to it."

Simply observing, she says, is something that both children and grown-ups today forget. Often the adults are as caught up in work and worries as kids are in their activities, and they no longer model behavior that's about taking time to be connected to the natural world.

"I was by a reservoir with my son, watching some herons, and suddenly this bald eagle swoops across the road. I'm staring at it, but people on the road just keep driving. I wanted to shout at them—don't you see that great big bird that just flew in front of you? Don't you want to stop and really look at it?"

What makes it more important than ever that we do stop and observe, she believes, is that caring for the planet grows from caring about it, from having an interest that sustains your heart, mind, or soul in a personal way. Feminist Gloria Steinem in the 1970s said the personal is the political. Beth is in agreement with this, as is every other bird lover I spoke to. Once a personal connection is made to a particular species—bird, mammal, tree, or what have you—you have the beginning of an environmental conscience.

Pete's sanctuary also gives many young people a place to make that connection, and their interest in birds then becomes action. One young girl told him what inspired her was that she knows that here, she's making a difference. His Massachusetts College of Liberal Arts intern, Tommy Flores, feels the same. A handsome young man with a friendly attitude and a lot of dark hair, he found the sanctuary in the mid-1990s, after he took a long road trip with a friend.

"I saw one dead bird after another on the road. Owls, hawks, all kinds of birds," he told me. "When we were going through Texas, I stopped to move one off the road, and when I touched it, it flapped its wing at me. It was still alive, so I bundled it up and put it in the car. It had a bump on its head and one leg was obviously injured, but it was feisty, looking at me like it was ready to go. My friend talked me into stopping at a vet's, and I finally gave in, against my better instincts. While he was taping up the leg, I asked him repeatedly what he'd do with it, and he reassured me over and over that they had plenty of places to take in injured owls. The owl kept looking at me, like it was saying 'don't leave me here,' but I listened to my head instead of my heart and I left it. The next day, when I called to find out how it was doing, the vet told me he'd euthanized it, because they had nowhere for it to go. I was furious, and I decided when

I got back to Massachusetts, I had to educate myself so that would never happen again. I found out about this place, and now here I am."

Pete refers to him as his adopted son. He volunteers time doing the same grunt work Pete does—hauling water and chopping wood—but he's also working on a newsletter for the sanctuary, excited to be doing something that's both positive and possible In a world that seems to be run by corporate interests

Dear Nancy and peter,

thank you for letting us come to see all the Birds. it was fun, exiting and informative. My favorite part was walkin with the Emus.

from
Emme

STUDENTS WRITE TO PETE.

and government red tape, both impervious to human or animal needs, a newsletter or ten dollars for Pete actually has an impact.

That, I think, is one of the more subtle but incredibly important gifts of the sanctuary. My college students these days often express a profound sense of disenfranchisement. The world to them is made up of huge corporate interests, and nothing they say or do can affect what happens in their lives. Companies will go

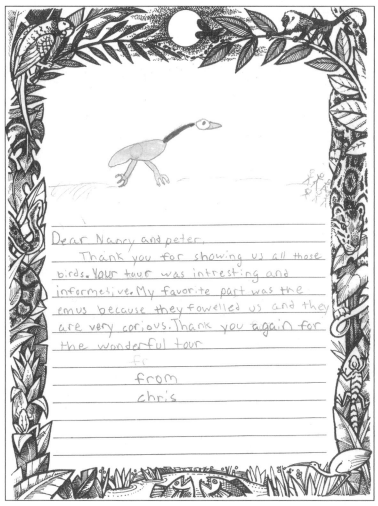

Dear Nancy and peter,
    Thank you for showing us all those
birds. Your tour was intresting and
informetive. My favorite part was the
emus because they fowelled us and they
are very corious. Thank you again for
the wonderful tour
                    fr
            from
            chris

STUDENTS WRITE TO PETE.

broke and the CEOs will still get millions, while their own parents are being laid off. Change, they think, is simply not possible.

But at the bird sanctuary, working to create something good is not only possible, it's a way of life. When they go there, they get to see it in action.

Younger children also get to see that. Somewhere between two and three thousand school-age kids come through the sanctuary every year. Public schools bring them in for the tour, and they walk around filling out worksheets, learning about the birds in person instead of from a book. Girl Scouts and Boy Scouts come through, and Pete tells them stories about the birds, how they lived in the wild, how they were injured and ended up here. Sometimes they'll tear up, feeling for the creatures they're seeing. They ask questions, most often wanting to know what his favorite bird is, and he tells them he doesn't have a favorite because each one is special. After they leave, they'll send pictures they drew, and little notes that most often say, "Thank you for taking care of the birds."

He keeps all their notes. "Those are things I can't throw away. They're too precious."

He's found that visiting his place helps these children develop not just a love of birds, but also a more general empathy, and a whole new sense of responsibility. "They see that life isn't just a hurray-for-me thing," he says. "We can all make a difference."

"Dear Mr. Pete Dubacher," one child writes. "Thank you for the wonderful tour. My favorite bird was one of the parrots. It put its beak on the cage and moved its feet. Thank you for taking out the baby falcon and telling us about it. Thank you for taking care of all those birds."

 NINETEEN

Migration Home

A small day
with sun in it and mocking
   bird on the wire—child of light tossing streamers in
the wind calling keeraway keeraway keera
   way I will learn to be a song, sway
   cascading in a curling plate of ribbons piled high and drop
a pitch in rythm—ricordarse—
   I will hear you
in my chords rising from the lily threads of throat
   Oh anima mea, anima mea
   will learn to be a rolling wide bowl of silk moon
nocturning through the rocking aisles smiling like
   12 children row on row who listen, listen,
   listen to the wailing trees
   listen to the sky, the sifting tide
   the raging bands of rainbows.
Trill the strolling slopes of pigeon people
   and knit out sweaters of song on a small small day
with children, on the wire mocking—
   birds call keeraway, learn
   keeraway to be
   a song.

                              —B. Chepaitis, "Vocatus"

1 P.M., Berkshire Bird Paradise
I'VE GOT MY BAGS out of the foofy room and back in my car,
as I get ready to head out. I'll be back here again, many times,

but for now I have to get back home. We have company coming for dinner, and I have some schoolwork to do before the week starts. When I find Pete to let him know, he tells me his father wants to see me first. "You have time?" he asks.

"I wanted to thank them before I left. I was heading that way." I head toward the house, figuring it'll be a quick goodbye, and I'll be on my way.

When I get inside, I see a few teenagers gathered around the TV watching cartoons, and I smell something yummy. Plates are set at the table, and Christine beams at me as she arranges utensils *"just* so."

William turns to me. "Do you like risotto?" he asks.

He doesn't really want to *see* me. He wants to feed me.

"Absolutely," I say, and sit down.

The risotto is five star. The roast chicken that goes with it is perfect. Pete comes in for a moment and grins, "Oh yeah. I didn't tell you he had lunch, did I?"

"I should have guessed," I admit. "Your Dad's a great chef," I say—not flattering, just noting the facts.

"Everybody eats pretty good around here," Pete agrees. He's got that look on his face, like he's listening to what's happening outside, thinking of his next task. "Find me before you leave, okay?"

I tell him I will, and then he's off, outside, continuing the pre-winter ritual of packing things away. By January he'll be getting ready for spring, making sure the eagle's nesting sites are secure and getting them adjusted to them, hoping for eggs in April. Throughout the winter he'll tend to renovations that can't be done in spring and summer for lack of time. Winter may be more difficult in many ways, but it's also more focused. It's just his family and the birds, with no visitors to tend to.

When I finish my meal, Christine takes me over to show me her collection of memorabilia from a trip she made many years ago to the Holy Land. It's a small, personal shrine that speaks to and of her own bright, definite spirit. There are candles, photos, religious items. She touches them lovingly.

"I swam in the Dead Sea," she tells me, the memory making her face glow. "They have a place there where they cover you in mud, and then wash it away. You go in the water of the Dead Sea and you float."

I try to imagine her as a younger woman, slathered in mud, then resting in the salt water that holds you up without effort. "I felt changed by it," she says. "Purified."

She's a woman who appreciates the sacred. That, I suppose, is another facet of Pete's choices explained. He learned to live deeply, unafraid of mud. And he's made his own sacred space, right here, in Paradise.

I go back outside to say good-bye to Pete. He's opening one of the sheds, and standing inside it is a watercolor painting—a drifting of textured sky against green mountains, everything muted and blended to create an impression of solitary peace, held within the ongoing action of a lively sky.

"That's yours?" I ask.

"Yeah. That's one of mine. It's relaxing, painting. About the only thing that keeps me standing still."

Men who care for the earth and make art and love their daughters. There are good examples here for adults as well as children, in a broader way than I expected to find. For Pete, it's no big deal. He closes the shed door, and turns to me.

So you'll keep me posted? Let me know how it's going?" he asks.

"I will. I'll have more questions, I'm sure. I'll call."

He smiles. "I have a good feeling about this. I think there's great things that can happen here. And y'know, people are ready for a change. They know they have to pay attention to the earth. We've been neglecting it, everybody caught up in being afraid. But that's changing." He looks around, as if sniffing the air for a scent of that change.

By the time I reach my car, he's out of sight. Pete, ever hopeful, ever busy, is already on to the next task. The trick here is to keep moving.

 TWENTY

The Thing with Feathers

We put our minds together as one and thank all the Birds who move and fly about over our heads. The Creator gave them beautiful songs. Each day they remind us to enjoy and appreciate life. The Eagle was chosen to be their leader. To all the Birds—from the smallest to the largest—we send out joyful greetings and thanks.

Now our minds are as one.

—*Ohen:ton Karihwatehkwen* (*Words Before All Else*)
A Mohawk greeting to the Natural World

WHEN I ARRIVE HOME, the heron is in the pond, and I experience again the thrill of having a giant bird in my yard. He shifts, stabs into the water, comes up with something good to eat, and swallows it down. I think of the juvenile heron, my futile rescue attempt, but this time I don't feel discouraged by that. I see the value in the trying. That comes from spending time with Pete, who values the small lives of birds, each particular one something important to him.

I once heard Abenaki storyteller Joe Bruchac tell a story about taking an elder to an event. They were running late, but the elder kept insisting they stop because it was spring, and the peepers were hopping wildly across the road. They'd stop and he'd get out of the car, pick one up, and place it safely on the other side of the road. Eventually, Joe grew impatient, said something about being late. "We really have somewhere we have to get to," he said to the elder.

159

The man just looked at the frog in his hand. "So does he," he said, and put the frog safely out of harm's way.

This is what I've learned from writing this book, from spending time with people who love birds, from seeing Pete do his work every day. We must love, and since love is a verb, that love must be acted on every day, in ways large and small. Each loving act is valuable, immeasurably so, adding to the store of the world's good in ways that ripple out beyond our individual failure or success, well beyond what we can immediately perceive.

What Pete Dubacher does with birds every day, for example, creates not only a safe haven for almost two thousand creatures that have nowhere else to go. It also creates a taste of paradise for the people who visit, his life showing his visitors that paradise can look and be homemade, that it thrives on personal commitment more than monetary wealth, and while it takes a big effort to sustain, the recompense is extraordinary. His life shows what it means to truly love, and to live that love on a daily basis. He makes it seem possible, and what seems possible can become real for others.

"Thank you," I whisper to the heron in my pond.

Thank you, I whisper to Bill Danielson, who helped save a crow. Thank you, I whisper to Kevin Burner, who germinates bird droppings. Thank you, I say to Meg, and Georgi, and Stephanie and Dan Woldin, and more. Thank you, I whisper to my husband, who saw the small life of the heron, and knew we had to try. Thank you, I say to Emily Dickinson, who never saw her work published, but who kept writing anyway.

And thank you, I say to the young heron who stayed with me for a very short time. Thank you, I send out to the red-winged blackbirds in the woods, the bluebirds who visit now and then, the improbable hummingbirds and assertive chickadees. Thank you to bower birds, lyre birds, and grebes. Thank you, I say to Pete's eagles, hawks, and owls, emus, ravens, and turkey vultures. Thank you, I say to pigeons there, and everywhere.

Thanks for eating all those bugs, and cleaning up all that carrion. Thanks for brightening the winter, heralding the spring, and giving musical interest all seasons of the year. Thank you for the lessons and the beauty you so generously share. Thank you for the hope, and the taste of paradise you bring.

May the world appreciate you more and more.

The heron stands in the pond, afternoon sun backlighting its still figure. I give it a silent salute, and go inside.

EPILOGUE

I SPOKE WITH PETE throughout the winter, which was a long and difficult one in the northeast. There was hard frost and a snowstorm in October, and the cold settled in to stay from then on. On December 12, 2008, when a big icestorm hit the area, Pete's power was out for almost a week, and he had to run a generator, using forty gallons of gas a day to keep everyone warm. "This is a wake up call," he said. "Something I really have to address. We have to seriously get into some kind of better energy source." He's looking into geothermal heat and wind turbines, hoping to find something he can afford. He sees these kinds of moments as an opportunity to learn.

"It's easy to sit around and feel sorry for yourself," he says, "but you have to ask yourself, 'Okay, here's the problem. How do we fix it?"

That, of course, he gets from his parents. They grounded him in that kind of thinking early on. But now, as he heads into his sixties, he's also thinking ahead to what might happen beyond him for this sanctuary and the birds that rely on its continued existence.

Most of the people I spoke with said they couldn't imagine the Berkshire Bird Paradise without Pete. "It would take about twenty Pete's to replace just him," John Pipkin said. "He does the work of many people."

Pete expects to be here for the rest of his life, but he's also thought about what he'd like to see happen beyond him. "It'd be great if I could connect to a college or some other educational facility. This place is about education—learning about the birds, breeding and releasing them, and educating others. The best case scenario I can imagine is something that continues doing that."

That, of course, is something we all hope isn't necessary for many years. For the immediate future, he has a different kind of wish list, and it involves a new refrigerator to store bird food, green energy for the place, more helping hands to get the various building projects done.

While he seeks out that kind of long-term assistance, he continues adding to his sanctuary, with new building, and a few new customers. He's beginning an education program with girls in a local corrections facility, to help them find hope for their own lives in the feathers of his birds. The Victoria crown pigeon is sitting on an egg. An eagle couple looks like they're nesting. And he has some new guests—two African tortoises.

They look like something carved out of sandstone that happens to move. Pete says they're a lot more responsive and affectionate than he thought they'd be. "The male arrived first, and he kind of moped around—until the female got here. Then he perked right up."

I get to hang out with the tortoises while the Victoria crown pigeon they share space with investigates my leg, cooing and bowing to my sneaker.

THE PERKY TORTOISE.

"He's flirting," Pete tells me.

"Nice to know I can still inspire that," I reply.

As usual, the place is magic. I mean, how often do you get to hang out with giant tortoises while a strange bird flirts with you? I ask Pete if the lousy economy is affecting him, and he says that people have really come through for him, supporting his birds with a generosity that he finds deeply touching. The pigeon rescue groups are particularly active these days, and they're being backed by people like Mayor Bloomberg and Mary Tyler Moore. That's an encouraging sign to him. It means people are paying attention, and they care.

"But one thing I've learned. You always have to leave room for surprises," he says.

"Right," I agree. "Always be ready for disaster."

He stops, thinks. "Actually, I meant surprises. Like, years ago a woman came here with an injured Canadian goose, and just as she pulled in, the bird died. She was distraught. Really upset. Me and Betty Ann took some time to sit with her, and console her. You know. Just what anyone would do. But just the other day, I got a letter, telling me that woman left $2000 for the sanctuary. She remembered what happened. It meant something to her. That's what I meant by surprises."

I laugh, thinking of the difference between our worldviews. "You're an optimist, Pete. An authentic optimist."

"I better be," he chuckles. "If you're not, you won't last long in this kind of business."

Emily Dickinson said that hope is the thing with feathers. Maybe that's why Pete has so much of it, all based on experience.

Hope is alive and well at the Berkshire Bird Paradise. Long may it prosper.

BIRD PLACES—REAL AND VIRTUAL

THESE DAYS, an internet search will lead you to many different kinds of places for birdwatching, for hiking, for listening to the trees. New York State has its share, including a few I've visited.

THE PINE BUSH PRESERVE. This rather surprising landscape located in the heart of Albany represents one of the best remaining examples of an inland pine barrens ecosystem in the world. It's a gently rolling sand plain you'd expect to see in the southwest rather than upstate New York, and it's home to a unique diversity of animals and plants, including twenty rare species.

Thousands of people visit its 3,010 acres of protected land each year for outdoor recreation, research, nature study, and respite, and it is vigilantly maintained by citizens who have fought for it since 1978, when they were outraged that a supposedly public hearing about building development in the area was held in the middle of one of the worst blizzards the city has ever seen. The proposal to build went through, and the now very irate citizens organized the Pine Bush Preservation group and sued the city. They remained feisty, and that's paid off for all concerned. Recently, as a result of various litigations, they were able to reclaim a credit union building and create the Pine Bush Discovery Center, which is now used for educational purposes.

For more information, visit *www.pinebush.org,* or phone 518-456-0655.

FIVE RIVERS ENVIRONMENTAL EDUCATION CENTER. Located in Delmar, New York, this is another urban sanctuary, open since 1972 by the New York State Department of Environmental

Conservation. It has over 450 acres of broad fields, forests, and wetlands, and hosts over 115,000 visitors annually.

Here the DEC has conducted studies of the ruffed grouse, raised game species for release, and field tested new techniques in wildlife management, many of which put New York in the forefront of a growing national conservation movement. Now it provides many programs and services for individuals, families, and organized groups, including guided walks and demonstrations, workshops for teachers, youth, and school groups, and more. They also have a library, a visitor center, and, of course, many walking trails.

For more information, visit *www.dec.ny.gov/education/1835.html*, phone: 518-475-0291, or email: *5rivers@gw.dec.state.ny.us*.

MONTEZUMA NATIONAL WILDLIFE REFUGE. Situated at the northern end of Cayuga Lake, this refuge is in the middle of one of the most active flight lanes in the Atlantic Flyway. Located thirty-five miles west of Syracuse, its 7,068 acres range across three counties. The refuge boasts forty-three species of mammals, fifteen reptile species, and sixteen amphibian species in a variety of habitats, including forest, shrub, grassland, and marsh. The latter provides crucial habitat for migratory waterfowl and other birds during their spring and fall journeys. Here, Canada and snow gees can fill the sky, and all manner of ducks can be seen dabbling or diving, depending on their species inclination. Shallow marsh pools also attract herons, egrets, rails, bitterns, and grebes. The endangered black tern has recently returned to nest there as well, so this is a bird lister's heaven.

Montezuma also has had a rather unique experience with bald eagles, having been home to a nest that had a trio rather than a pair of eagles tending the young. Visitors have also witnessed eagles and ospreys duking it out on the wing over nesting sites, locking talons in midair to see who would keep one particular site.

They have plenty of programming here, and lots of land to walk around. For particulars, visit *www.fws.gov/r5mnwr*, or phone 315-568-5987.

There are plenty of other places to visit in the state. A good place to begin searching for spots near you is the Nature Conservancy: *www.nature.org/wherewework/northamerica/states/newyork/preserves* (phone: 518-690-7850).

Websites of Interest

BILL DANIELSON
He has a lovely website along with his regular newspaper columns. Find him at *speaking of nature.com*.

RICH GUTHRIE
He has a regular blog, which you can read here: *blog.timesunion.com/birding*.

CORNELL UNIVERSITY
They have a variety of bird programs and information on their site: *www.birds.cornell.edu*.

NEW YORK STATE DEPARTMENT OF ENVIRONMENTAL CONSERVATION
To find out more about what the DEC is up to, and to get useful links to other sites, go to *www.dec.ny.gov*.

FOR PIGEONS:
New York City Pigeon Rescue Central: *nycprc.org*.
If you have an urgent pigeon situation, you can call (212) 873-6030.

FOR TROPICALS:
Central New York Avian Rescue: *www.geocities.com/mcadamsbirdrescue/index*.
They take in and adopt out tropicals from parrots to Macaws.

BIRD REHABILITATORS, NEW. YORK STATE:
If you're in New York State and have an injured or abandoned bird you need help with, New York State keeps a list of licensed animal and bird rehabilitators listed by regions on their website: *www.nyswrc.org/rehabbers.html*.
If you're interested in becoming licensed, or taking classes to learn about rehabilitating wildlife, Beth Bidwell recommends

North Country Wild Care, located in Warrensburg, New York. They hold classes at Saratoga Public Library, have lists of wildlife veterinarians, and more. Visit their website at *www.northcountry-wildcare.org.*

For information on classes, phone Lisa Penistan at 518-494-4891 or email: *whstarmorganfarm@yahoo.com.*

For Further Fun and Education

I watched the PBS series *The Life of Birds* as part of my research for this book, and I can't recommend it enough. Your library may have a copy of the series, or you can learn how to get it at *PBS.org.*

If you want to participate in the Christmas Bird Count, or just find out more about it, go to *www.audobon.org.* There you can find information on your local Audobon branch. For information about participating in the New York State Breeding Bird Atlas, go to *www.dec.ny.gov/animals/7312.html.* Or just call up the New York State Department of Environmental Conservation at 518-402-8919, and tell them Barbara sent you.

BIBLIOGRAPHY

Habegger, Larry, and Amy G. Carlson, eds. *The Gift of Birds: True Encounters with Avian Spirits.* San Francisco: Travelers' Tales, Inc., 1999.

Allen, Paula Gunn. *Grandmothers of the Light: A Medicine Woman's Sourcebook,* Boston: Beacon, 1991.

Ponting, Clive. *A Green History of the World.* New York: Penguin, 1992.

Blechman, Andrew D. *Pigeons.* New York: Grove Atlantic, 2006.

Gingras, Pierre. *The Secret Lives of Birds.* Ontario: Firefly Books, 1995.

Rothenberg, David. *Why Birds Sing: A Journey into the Mystery of Bird Song.* New York: Basic Books, 2005.

1	31	61	91	121	151	181	211	241	271	301	331
2	32	62	92	122	152	182	212	242	272	302	332
3	33	63	93	123	153	183	213	243	273	303	333
4	34	64	94	124	154	184	214	244	274	304	334
5	35	65	95	125	155	185	215	245	275	305	335
6	36	66	96	126	156	186	216	246	276	306	336
7	37	67	97	127	157	187	217	247	277	307	337
8	38	68	98	128	158	188	218	248	278	308	338
9	39	69	99	129	159	189	219	249	279	309	339
10	40	70	100	130	160	190	220	250	280	310	340
11	41	71	101	131	161	191	221	251	281	311	341
12	42	72	102	132	162	192	222	252	282	312	342
13	43	73	103	133	163	193	223	253	283	313	343
14	44	74	104	134	164	194	224	254	284	314	344
15	45	75	105	135	165	195	225	255	285	315	345
16	46	76	106	136	166	196	226	256	286	316	346
17	47	77	107	137	167	197	227	257	287	317	347
18	48	78	108	138	168	198	228	258	288	318	348
19	49	79	109	139	169	199	229	259	289	319	349
20	50	80	110	140	170	200	230	260	290	320	350
21	51	81	111	141	171	201	231	261	291	321	351
22	52	82	112	142	172	202	232	262	292	322	352
23	53	83	113	143	173	203	233	263	293	323	353
24	54	84	114	144	174	204	234	264	294	324	354
25	55	85	115	145	175	205	235	265	295	325	355
26	56	86	116	146	176	206	236	266	296	326	356
27	57	87	117	147	177	207	237	267	297	327	357
28	58	88	118	148	178	208	238	268	298	328	358
29	59	89	119	149	179	209	239	269	299	329	359
30	60	90	120	150	180	210	240	270	300	330	360